Divine Analogies

*Reflections On Seeking God And
Walking With Jesus*

Volume 2

52 Weekly Reflections

Charles D. (Chuck) Vollmer

Published by Jobenomics Publishing, Vienna, Virginia, United States.

ISBN: 979-8-9938170-1-9

Library of Congress Control Number: Pending

Scripture quotations, unless otherwise noted, are from the Holy Bible. Public domain.

This book is part of the Divine Analogies Series, which explores parallels between spiritual principles, economic systems, and community development.

Printed in the United States of America.

First Edition.

Visit our websites:

https://DivineAnalogies.org

https://Jobenomics.org

Divine Analogies Volume 2
Introduction

Reflections On Seeking God and Walking with Jesus

Divine Analogies, Volume 2 continues the journey begun in Volume 1—52 weekly reflections on what it means to seek God and walk with Jesus amid the ordinary, often unpredictable realities of modern life. These essays arise from my own story: a five-decade-long traveler—at times a straggler—on the road of faith. They are offered not as lectures but as personal reflections, written to encourage those seeking direction, asking hard questions, or wondering how biblical truths apply to daily challenges.

My journey with Christ began in earnest at age 30. At that time, I had achieved much that the world counts as success—a decorated combat pilot, a promising career, a young family—but I felt an inner emptiness I could not explain. One restless night, I cried out, "If You are real, God, prove Yourself." He did. That moment marked the beginning of a lifelong journey during which I have learned that God meets me where I am — often in the midst of striving and brokenness — and patiently draws me ever closer to Him.

This second volume reflects that ongoing journey. Each essay combines Scripture, vivid metaphors, and real-life experiences—from flying combat missions to leading community development initiatives—to show how eternal truths can be grasped in practical ways. Reflections such as "Imperfection as a Reflection," "Jesus as a Fire Chief," and "Holy Spirit as

My Superpower" illustrate how faith speaks to both the heart and the demands of daily life.

The central theme of this volume is that faith is an ongoing walk rather than a one-time event. It invites readers to return daily to Christ as their source of strength, to let the Holy Spirit shape character and choices, and to live with humility, forgiveness, loyalty, discernment, and hope. These qualities are not abstract ideals but daily practices that equip us to be light-bearers in a world often marked by hurry, conflict, and distraction.

My prayer is that these reflections will encourage others, as they have encouraged me, to pause, listen for God's voice, and recognize His presence in the ordinary as well as the extraordinary. I learned that transformation does not come all at once but unfolds along the journey—sometimes slow and uneven—yet always guided by the One who calls us to walk with Him.

God created me to do good works in Jesus, emitting the aroma of Christ and the fruits of the Holy Spirit that are pleasing to our Heavenly Father. After decades of progress, I think I am becoming the person God intended me to be. However, this transformation will take an eternity to finish.

Chuck Vollmer

Table of Contents

Jesus' Mission as a Foregone Conclusion

The Incarnation was a pivotal event, not merely a rescue mission but a demonstration of divine strategy against evil. While the established reasons for Jesus' coming—salvation, revelation, and fulfillment of the law—remain foundational, they gain a sharp, dramatic focus in an ongoing spiritual war with Satan. Jesus, as God, was always the ultimate victor; the conclusion was, in fact, foregone. Unbeknownst to Satan, Jesus's primary reason for coming and ultimate goal was not to defeat Satan but to conquer death itself.

The true purpose of Jesus' first coming in physical form was to publicly, legally, and demonstrably dismantle Satan's claim over humanity, and, crucially, to show vulnerable humans how to overcome that claim for themselves. The Bible describes Earth as a contested testing ground. Satan, banished but still active and granted temporary rule, was highly successful in corrupting human souls. The prior interventions, such as the Flood and the confounding of the Tower of Babel, were interim measures—handicaps placed on Satan's recruitment efforts.

The core of this spiritual warfare was Jesus' Incarnation. Jesus, being God and all-powerful, voluntarily chose to submit to denying His royal power as a tactical necessity for a fair demonstration. He had to face the enemy on the same terms as humanity—relying not on inherent divine might, but on Holy Spirit power and obedience to the Father. This act served as a visible blueprint for humanity, showing us exactly how to access God's power to resist evil.

The first confrontation was the temptation in the wilderness. Satan's offer—his earthly kingdom for service—was a direct challenge to the legitimacy of God's authority on earth. Jesus' successful resistance signaled to Satan and his fallen angels that their time was indeed up and that Spirit-filled humans could overcome their temptations.

Throughout His ministry, Jesus mitigated Satan's recruitment by healing, casting out demons, and preaching a path of righteousness. Demons recognized Him immediately, a sign of their fear and inevitable defeat. The path Jesus laid out was explicitly described as a treacherous, narrow gate. This suggests His primary goal wasn't universal mass enrollment, but the assembly of a disciplined, resilient core—those willing to forego the temporary, material rewards offered by Satan's earthly system in exchange for eternal union with God.

Suffering, trials, and the eventual Crucifixion weren't just atonement; they were the ultimate act of resistance within the framework of spiritual warfare. Jesus proved that the fear of death, which the devil wielded, held no power over one who perfectly obeyed the Father. His victory wasn't just *for* us; it was a lesson on how to resist, endure, and ultimately triumph with the power of the Holy Spirit. The conclusion was foregone, but the lesson had to be lived.

Spirituality as a Calling

Spirituality is not merely a personal choice—it is a calling. It is an invitation, extended by God, that often precedes conscious recognition. Some hear a whisper and turn to Him, while others, like me, deeply entrenched in worldly pursuits, require a dramatic encounter. My experience speaks to the reality that God was calling me long before I formally accepted Christ at age 30.

My earliest recollections of this calling date back to my childhood. One Sunday morning in Lincoln, Nebraska, I found myself walking alone to a church half a mile away while my parents slept in. This was not a Samuel-like moment, where a voice called in the night and Eli instructed him to say, "Speak, LORD, for Your servant is listening." (1 Samuel 3:9). Yet, it was something—an inexplicable pull toward God's house, toward something beyond my understanding.

Later, at age 16, in Pennsylvania, I trained as an acolyte in the Episcopal Church. I recall a priest telling me that no one enters ministry without a calling. One particular moment stands out: during a service, as I retrieved the bread and wine, I felt an overwhelming spiritual presence, a force so strong that the priest came to check on me. These moments marked something deeper—whispers from God, calling me even as I remained largely agnostic.

By the time I was 30, life had given me everything that should have brought me fulfillment. I was a decorated fighter pilot, an academy graduate, married to my high school sweetheart (and still am), and very prideful. From the outside, my life looked complete. And yet, within, I felt hollow—an emptiness growing into a darkness that no earthly achievement could fill.

One restless night, unable to escape this void, I walked into the open air and cried out in frustration: "If You are real, God, prove Yourself!" He did.

What followed was a spiritual battle—two months of wrestling between darkness and light. I did not realize it at the time, but this tug-of-war was real, culminating in a divine encounter: an apparition of Jesus Himself. In that moment, He told me it was time to make a choice. I asked only one question: "Do I have to quit being a warrior and become a holy roller?" He smiled and answered, "I want you for you." No conditions, no mandates—just acceptance. In that moment, my answer came naturally: "Okay, I'm in." Jesus vanished, and the spiritual fog lifted at 2 AM. Four hours later, my Christian mentor called. She had been awakened at the very same time and had prayed for me without knowing why—an undeniable confirmation of what had transpired.

Not every calling comes with dramatic encounters. Most hear a gentle whisper and, in faith, respond. For me, entrenched so deeply in the enemy's camp, that whisper was not enough—it took the direct intervention of Christ Himself. Yet, in every calling, one truth remains: He calls each of us in a way that meets us precisely where we are.

You as Before Me

One of the most profound lessons Jesus taught was the principle of submission, which involves placing the Father's will above personal desires.

In the Garden of Gethsemane, facing the agony of crucifixion, Jesus prayed, "Not my will, but Yours be done" (Luke 22:42). That moment wasn't weakness—it was divine strength. It was the embodiment of "YOU before me." Jesus didn't just teach this; He lived it. And He instructed His disciples to do the same: to seek the Holy Spirit's guidance in His absence, to wait, to discern, and to act appropriately and decisively.

As a long-time follower of Christ, I've come to understand that this posture—putting God's will and others' needs before my own—isn't just a spiritual concept. It's a daily discipline. One that shows up in the most ordinary places: the grocery store, the workplace, the sidewalk. I'v

e learned to be respectful to all people, even those who show me none in

return. That's not a boast—it's a testimony. The Spirit has trained my heart to recognize discontented and angry souls from a distance. Not to avoid them, but to approach them with kindness and understanding.

Sometimes, all it takes is a smile. A simple "hello." A gesture that says, "I see you." However, I'm not naïve. I don't engage recklessly. God has given me discernment—a gift that helps me know when to speak and when to stay silent, when to lean in and when to walk away. Proverbs 1:5 says, "Let the discerning get guidance." The Holy Spirit is my counselor and guide, just like the guide that Jesus relied on when dealing with the Romans, Pharisees, and his fellow citizens who wanted to do harm or kill Him.

Discernment is the Holy Spirit's whisper in the noise of human emotion and the chaos of the world. It's the pause before the reaction. It's the difference between confrontation and compassion. Jesus modeled this perfectly. He didn't treat every person the same. He didn't respond to every insult with a rebuke. Sometimes, He answered with a question. Sometimes, He walked away. And sometimes, He wept.

In my own walk, I've come to see that "YOU before me" is not just about obedience to God—it's about honoring the image of God in others. Even with anger. Even with disrespect. Even in those who seem unreachable. Because grace isn't earned—it's extended. And when I choose to reflect that grace, I'm not just being polite. I'm emulating my mentor.

So, whether I'm writing, creating, or simply living, I try to keep this posture: YOU as before me, God's will before mine, and Others' dignity before my pride. The Spirit's leading before my impulse. It's not always easy. But it's always well worth the effort.

Three as One, Part 1

A Lighthearted Reflection on the Trinity

The Christian concept of the Trinity has always been a puzzle for me, even after decades of walking with Jesus. To make sense of this profound mystery, I sometimes picture the Holy Trinity as "The Three Amigos," a playful image based on the 1986 American Western comedy that doesn't diminish their majesty but helps me see them as a unified team I'm eager to serve. As a former fighter pilot, I also envision this awesome Threesome as a three-ship formation, soaring in perfect sync, invincible against any foe. These lighthearted analogies draw me closer to God, making their unity relatable and inspiring.

The doctrine of the Trinity teaches that God is one essence in three persons: Father, Jesus, and Spirit. Each is fully God, sharing the exact divine nature, yet distinct in role. The Father is the source, the Son is begotten and incarnate, and the Spirit proceeds from both. They are one God, not three, coequal and eternal, a truth that stretches my mind. The Shield of the Trinity, a medieval symbol, helps me visualize this: three nodes for Father, Son, and Spirit connect to a central "God," each marked "is" to affirm their divinity, while "is not" lines between them highlight their distinctness.

My "Three Amigos" image portrays the Holy Trinity as a band of companions working in joyful harmony. The Father sets the plan with wisdom, the Son executes it with courage, and the Spirit infuses it with energy, like friends on a shared adventure. Similarly, my pilot's mind sees them as a three-ship formation, each person a jet flying in tight precision. The Father charts the mission, the Son breaks through the fray, and the Spirit covers the flanks, guiding with uncanny skill. These images, though imperfect, make the Trinity feel like a team I can cheer for, not a distant theological riddle.

The Shield's triangular design, often encircled, suggests dynamic movement, like planes banking in unison. There's no hierarchy, only unity in diversity. I sometimes focus too much on Jesus' humanity, sidelining the Father's authority or the Spirit's guidance, but the Shield reminds me they're inseparable. Each person's role—Father as planner, Son as redeemer, Spirit as empowerer—interlocks perfectly, inviting me into God's mission.

These images reshape how I approach faith. Picturing the Trinity as a lively, coordinated team inspires me to live with purpose, reflecting God's unity in my actions. Whether as amigos sharing laughter or pilots executing a flawless maneuver, they show me what teamwork means.

These analogies stir my heart, making the Trinity more than a doctrine to memorize. They're a living reality, a team that welcomes my participation. My "Three Amigos" and three-ship images spark awe and a desire to serve. I may never fully grasp the Trinity's depths, but picturing Them as a united, purposeful squad fuels my gratitude and motivates me to join Their ranks.

Three as One, Part 2

The Crucifixion's Dark Unity

The Trinity—one God in three persons—has long eluded my grasp. My lighthearted analogies, like Three Amigos or a three-ship formation in Part 1, collapse under the weight of the crucifixion's horror. In this dark analogy, I envision the Father, Son, and Holy Spirit enduring the crucifixion together, united against a satanic parody of the Trinity: Satan, the anti-God dragon; the beast, the Antichrist; and the false prophet, the anti-Spirit. Though imperfect, this vision makes their sacrifice visceral.

I picture the Trinity at a small round table, crafting a plan to redeem fallen angels and humans—not as distant rulers, but as redeemers. Scripture hints at this divine strategy that uses a series of trials and tribulations to test and reveal creation's preferences for God's light or the darkness of evil. To give humans any chance of salvation, Jesus volunteered to become fully human, showing humankind the path to success. Through kenosis, Jesus emptied Himself of divine privilege, relying on the Father's strength via the Holy Spirit to face the enemy. This self-emptying made the test not only fair but a model for humanity to follow.

The crucifixion is where the cost of this plan becomes unbearable. The Father and Spirit, unified in essence with Jesus, fully experienced His agony.

Though scripture doesn't detail how the Father and Spirit experienced it, I imagine Them fully conscious of every moment, even as Jesus' body entered shock. The Father and Spirit felt every curse, slap, whip, and nail pain, not lessened by distance, but intensified by love for Jesus.

I imagine the Father watching the crucifixion with a fury that could have shattered the earth. The insolence of those mocking His Son and spitting in the face of the One He sent was mind-bending. Each act of cruelty—the leather whips with barbs, the twisted crown, and the nails that pinned Jesus' hands and feet to blood-soaked wood—was a provocation against the Almighty and heavenly host.

The Spirit, equally distraught, did not soothe but restrained. Not the Son—Jesus was already surrendered—but the Father, whose justice could have incinerated Golgotha with a word. The fact that HE held back is not weakness—it is terrifying strength. The wrath of God, fully justified, was suspended for the sake of the plan.

This reflection transforms the Trinity from abstraction to visceral reality. Their willingness to suffer as one, for my sake, stirs a love no theology alone could evoke. Father's restraint, Son's sacrifice, Spirit's guidance—each role endears the Trinity to me individually and as a whole.

I can't fathom how and why they endured the crucifixion, but this mystery drives me to honor the Trinity's three-as-one sacrifice. Their unified stand against darkness calls me not just to marvel, but to trust and serve with the same resolve.

Satiated as in God

There are moments after a good meal when I lean back and feel completely satiated. My hunger's quelled, my body's satisfied, and I'm not looking for anything more. It's simple, human fullness. Lately, I've caught myself wondering how that same sense of being filled points to something deeper—how God meets me in places I didn't even know were empty until they began to ache.

When loneliness creeps in, anxiety tightens my chest, or weariness drains me, I've noticed the Holy Spirit whispering to me softly, not as a distant figure, but as a presence within as my counselor, caregiver, and conscience. More importantly, He links me to Jesus, who is not only my Savior, but also my master, mentor, and friend. Shifting my focus to God doesn't erase every problem, but it steadies me. My restlessness eases, and I sense a kind of satisfaction I could never manufacture on my own.

But just like physical food, spiritual satiation doesn't last. A hearty dinner barely carries me through the day, and one moment with God only sustains me temporarily. On both accounts, I have to repeat the process daily, sometimes multiple times a day, to refill or top off. Paul's words in Ephesians 5:18 remind me of that rhythm: "Be filled with the Spirit," not once, but often. Romans 15:13 echoes the same idea that God fills me with joy and peace so that hope rises when life presses in.

Jesus' invitation in John 7 is also instructive: "If anyone is thirsty, let him come to me and drink." He was speaking of the Spirit, the living water that flows into parched souls. I've known that dryness, and I've known the relief of quenching a thirsty soul. The Spirit doesn't give me a quick fix; He nourishes me slowly, like living water seeping into desert soil. Galatians 5 points to what grows from that nourishment, fruits (love, joy, and peace) that show He's at work.

The more I reflect, the more I see how fleeting worldly satiation can be. It's like reaching for junk food when I'm hungry—quick, convenient, and temporarily satisfying, but ultimately leaving me sluggish or craving more. I've reached for those substitutes plenty of times—success, distraction, noise. But none of them last. By contrast, the Spirit's filling is more like manna from heaven. It's not excess; it's not indulgence. It's enough. Just what I need for today.

Romans 14 reminds me that the kingdom isn't about food or drink but about righteousness, peace, and joy in the Spirit. That's the kind of fullness that holds, even when circumstances don't. Acts 13 shows the early disciples "filled with joy and with the Holy Spirit" despite their challenges. I wonder if that's the same resilience I feel when I let God fill me rather than chasing lesser things.

In the end, satiation in God isn't a one-time feast. It's a cycle of daily return. Each time I reach for Him, He gives just enough—not to the point of excess, but to the point of peace. And that, I've come to realize, is the only fullness that truly lasts.

God as LORD-Jesus as Lord

I believe that introducing somebody correctly is essential. It is also vital when witnessing God the Father and Jesus.

To new believers and non-believers, the use of the title "God" can be confusing, as it is unclear whom I'm referring to—The Almighty Father or Jesus the Christ (the Anointed One). The word "God" can refer to the Trinity collectively or to Jesus' divinity, but it most often points to the

Father. Without clarity, I risk misrepresenting the relationship between the Father and the Son, as well as the reverence due to each.

When Scripture refers to the Father as LORD—in all caps—it is translating the divine name YHWH (Yahweh), the covenant name revealed to Moses. This is not a generic title; it is the name of the eternal, self-existent One. In passages like Isaiah 63:16, I read, "You, LORD, are our Father, our Redeemer from of old is your name." Here, the Father is both LORD and Father—sovereign and intimate. He is the source, the initiator, the One who sent the Son.

Jesus, on the other hand, is often referred to as Lord—capital "L," lowercase "ord"—a title of authority, divinity, and kingship. Philippians 2:11 says, "Every tongue will confess that Jesus Christ is Lord, to the glory of God the Father." This distinction is not a hierarchy of value, but a revelation of roles. The Father glorifies the Son, and the Son submits to the Father—not out of inferiority, but out of perfect unity.

When Paul writes in 2 Corinthians 1:3, "Blessed be the God and Father of our Lord Jesus Christ," I see a careful distinction. The Father is God—the source and head—and Jesus is Lord—the revealed Son, the Anointed One. This doesn't diminish Jesus' divinity. John 1:1 affirms, "In the beginning was the Word, and the Word was with God, and the Word was God." Jesus is fully divine, possessing all the attributes of God the Father. But He is not the Father. He is the Son, eternally begotten, not made.

So, when I say, "Jesus is God," I am affirming that Jesus is one with the Father in essence, nature, and glory. But I must also be careful not to collapse the three entities of the Trinity into one indistinct being. The Father is not the Son, and the Son is not the Spirit. Yet they are one God—unified in will, purpose, and being.

When I am asked if Jesus is God, my answer is "Yes." If appropriate, I tell them that when I speak of God, I tend to reserve the use of "God" to identify only my heavenly Father. When I talk of Jesus, to honor His divinity without confusing His personhood, I call Him either Lord or my Lord and Savior. If this person is still interested in what I believe, I mention my relationship with the Father who sent me, the Son who saved me, and the Spirit who indwells me. Each name matters. Each role matters. And clarity honors the truth I've been entrusted to share.

Imperfection as a Reflection

I used to view my imperfections as obstacles—flaws to be corrected, weaknesses to be overcome. But over time, I've come to see that my shortcomings are not merely signs of failure; they are reflections of something more profound. They reveal my need for God's grace, showing me how much I depend on Him for cleansing, renewal, and transformation.

As Paul wrote in 2 Corinthians 12:9, "My grace is sufficient for you, for my power is made perfect in weakness." My imperfections do not separate me from God—they allow His strength to be made visible in my life.

This understanding became even clearer to me through a simple but heartfelt exchange with my twin granddaughters. Almost every time I see them, I ask them two questions: *"What do I like about you?"* And *"What don't I like about you?"* Without hesitation, they always answer *everything* and *nothing*, respectively. Their confidence in my sincerity is complete—they know they are loved, not because they are perfect, but simply because they are mine.

The Holy Spirit showed me that this is how God sees me when His Son cleanses me daily. As Isaiah 1:18 says, "Though your sins are like scarlet, they shall be as white as snow." My failures do not define me—God's love and redemption do.

Every day, I fall short—making mistakes and failing in ways both big and small. It can be frustrating, but I am learning that God does not call me to be flawless; He calls me to be faithful. Ecclesiastes 1:14 warns that chasing after the wind is futile, and in many ways, pursuing perfection feels the same. Instead of fixating on unattainable standards, I am trying to focus on God's will, trusting that His purpose is greater than my failures.

The Bible is filled with people who were far from perfect—David, Peter, and Paul—yet God used them in powerful ways. Their lives remind me that imperfection does not disqualify anyone from being used for His glory. Romans 8:28 assures me that "in all things, God works for the good of those who love him." Even my shortcomings can be used to bring Him glory. When I acknowledge my weaknesses, I find that I am better able to extend grace to others, recognizing that, like me, they are imperfect yet loved.

God's love is unconditional. He accepts me as I am, yet He also invites me to grow and be transformed through Him. The more I surrender my desires to His, the more I see His hand at work in my life.

Ultimately, it is not about erasing imperfection, but about seeing it as a reflection of God's unending grace. Through Him, my flaws do not condemn me—they remind me of my need for Him, and they make His love shine even brighter.

Fasting as Isaiah

It seems to me that fasting was far more central to spiritual life in the time of Christ than it is today. Back then, it wasn't just a discipline—it was a declaration. A way to say, "My appetite does not rule me, but by my allegiance." I've tried fasting in the traditional sense—skipping meals, setting aside comforts—but I'll admit, it never became a regular rhythm for me. Outside of Lent, when I've forsaken a bad habit or two, my attempts have been sporadic at best.

Still, I've never let go of the conviction that fasting matters. Not as a performance, but as a posture. A way of humbling myself before the Almighty. And in that quiet pursuit, the Holy Spirit led me to Isaiah 58—a passage that reshaped my understanding of what it means to fast in a way that pleases God.

Verse 5 speaks of humility: "Is this the kind of fast I have chosen, only a day for a man to humble himself?" That struck me. Fasting isn't just about abstaining—it's about yielding to God's will and purpose for His glory, not mine. Not outwardly, but inwardly. It's about recognizing that I am not the center of the story, and that my strength is borrowed, not earned.

Verse 6 goes deeper: "Is not this the kind of fasting I have chosen: to loose the chains of injustice... to set the oppressed free?" That's not a metaphor. That's the mission. Fasting, in God's eyes, is about rightness, fairness, equity, and integrity. It's about stepping into the mess and lifting burdens that aren't mine, simply because He wants us to respect His will by caring for others.

Verse 7 calls me to action: "Is it not to share your food with the hungry and to provide the poor wanderer with shelter?" That's not poetic—it's Jesus. And it's where I've found my footing. Over the last fifteen years, God has strengthened me—not just spiritually, but structurally—to build something that reflects this kind of fast. A nonprofit that helps underserved communities start micro and self-employed businesses. It's often unappreciated work to help beleaguered communities that have lost hope, but it's rewarding and righteous because it's rooted in Isaiah's call.

Verse 10 reminds me to open my heart: "If you spend yourselves on behalf of the hungry..." That phrase—spend yourselves—isn't about money. It's about energy, time, and presence. It's about being poured out, not just filled up. And verse 11? That's the promise: "The Lord will guide you always; He will satisfy your needs... He will strengthen your frame." I've felt that. Not in dramatic ways, but in quiet endurance. In the ability to carry a heavier load, not for myself.

I do this kind of fasting. And I believe, with all humility, that Isaiah 58's version of fasting—now my version—is pleasing to God.

Graven as on His Hands

"I have graven thee upon the palms of my hands." Isaiah 49:16

This verse has always struck me as both intimate and sobering. The image of God engraving His people on the palms of His hands is not poetic fluff— it's a covenant that can't be casually erased. It's cutting deep, leaving scars. And when I think of scars, I can't help but think of Jesus.

The Father's words in Isaiah echo forward to the crucifixion, where Jesus

bore the nails in His hands (actually wrists). His scars are not reminders of pain; they are proof of promise. The Israelites were graven on the Father's hands, and I believe I am too, on Jesus's. Not metaphorically, but spiritually and eternally. And just as the Holy Spirit engraved Jesus on my hands, I sense that He also engraved Jesus on my heart. It's a two-way bond. Not mystical but real.

But real doesn't mean easy. Bonds stretch. I've lived long enough to know that even with the best intentions, I miss the mark. I stumble. I veer off the path. I don't lie anymore—not knowingly—but I still fall short. And when I do, I feel the tension in that bond. As a rubber band pulled too far, I worry it might snap. Not because God is unfaithful, but because I am prone to sin. Paul understood this tension. He ran the race with discipline, knowing that he wasn't guaranteed the prize unless he finished well.

Jesus promised never to break the bond. The Father endorsed that promise. They don't lie. They don't forget. But I've seen how quickly backsliding can happen. It's not a dramatic fall—it's a slippery slope. One moment I'm listening, the next I can't hear His voice. The world's distractions are loud, seductive, and relentless. And if I'm not vigilant, I slide. I've felt that darkness. I've tasted the silence. It's frightening.

The parables warn us: ten bridesmaids, only five ready; three servants, only two faithful; seeds sown, only some rooted. These aren't just stories—they're diagnostics. They show how easy it is to drift, to lose grace, not because God withdraws it, but because we choose something else—the world over heaven. I've seen it. And I don't want it to happen to me, as it has to others.

Isaiah's structure reinforces this. Chapters 1–39 warn of judgment. Chapters 40–55 offer messianic hope. Chapters 56–66 envision renewal. Isaiah 49 sits in the middle—hope wrapped in warning. The engraving on God's hands is a promise, but also a call to vigilance. It points to Jesus's sacrifice and His return. It reminds me that while He holds me, I must hold on to Him.

So, I strive—not perfectly, but persistently. Because I believe the bond is real, and I don't want to stretch it to the point of breaking due to my own negligence. I am determined to finish the race and be among the bridesmaids with oil, the servants with returns, the seeds that bear fruit. Why? Because I am graven on His hands, and He is engraved on my heart.

Blessed as a Pauper

The word *pauper* isn't heard much anymore. It feels antiquated, almost  literary. Yet it leapt off the page as I read Luke 21—the story of the poor widow who gave two copper coins. Jesus said she gave more than all the wealthy donors combined. That struck me. She was a pauper. Yet she was blessed because she gave out of her lack.

Jesus opens His Sermon on the Mount with a similar paradox: "Blessed are the poor in spirit." Those who come empty, not full. It runs counter to our instincts. We usually associate blessing with fullness—overflowing bank accounts, packed schedules, and thriving congregations. But God seems to favor the hungry. The ones who know, deep down, that they are in need. Hunger fuels movement. Emptiness makes room. And in that space, God shows up. He fills the void with His Spirit, His power, His grace. He blesses what is surrendered.

Today, a pauper is typically defined as someone living in extreme poverty, with an income of less than $2 a day. That includes over 800 million people worldwide, according to the World Bank. Expand the threshold to $8 a day, and nearly half the planet—3.7 billion people—qualify.

From where I sit, the enemy (Satan) is exploiting the economic divide between the poor and the prosperous, feeding resentment and violence. In a world increasingly shaken, it often feels like he's winning the war for hearts, minds, and souls.

As I look back over the last forty years, I see how Jesus was preparing me—sometimes in ways I didn't understand—to engage both material and spiritual poverty. Through military and business endeavors, I witnessed firsthand the depths of deprivation in dozens of nations. I was tasked with helping to lead one of seven consortia that privatized 70% of the Soviet Union's state-run economy, giving rise to millions of firms from the wreckage of a collapsed regime.

Today, I have the honor of founding and leading Jobenomics, a nonprofit dedicated to grassroots job and business creation. Over the last 15 years, we've launched more than 100 community chapters across four continents—each led by local citizens who believe that economic empowerment is essential to breaking the cycle of generational poverty and overcoming social mobility barriers.

But this story isn't about me or what I've done. It's about what Christ has done through a willing, imperfect vessel. My part was to remain open. To say yes. And in that surrender, I've found peace. I've found purpose. I've come to believe that even the smallest offering, when given in faith, is seen and treasured by God.

I've learned I don't need to be flawless. I don't need to be fully equipped. What matters is the posture of my heart—being willing to give whatever I have, no matter how small, and trusting Him to multiply it.

Discipleship as in Standing in the Gap

Ezekiel 22:30 says, "I looked for someone among them who would build up the wall and stand before me in the gap on behalf of the land so I would not have to destroy it, but I found no one." That verse doesn't just speak—it convicts. As a former combat-tested fighter pilot, I understand the importance of holding a line. In combat, gaps are fatal. In faith, they're just as dangerous.

Discipleship, for me, is standing in the gap. It's not about having all the answers or being the loudest voice—it's about being present when it matters most. It's about interceding when the world is unraveling. Today, I see corruption, rage, and violence tearing through America and beyond. The walls are breached. I've watched good people choose inaction over conviction. When that happens, evil takes hold with ever-increasing intensity and maliciousness. Evil begets evil with compound interest rates.

I've seen this not just in war zones, but also in quiet places, like boardrooms and even churches. The silence of the righteous can be deafening. Proverbs 24:11-12 warns believers not to ignore those being led to slaughter. Any inaction or procrastination is a sin, an anathema to God.

Scripture records many notable accounts of standing in the gap. Moses did it when he pleaded for Israel after the golden calf (Exodus 32:11-14). Phinehas did it when he stopped a plague through righteous zeal (Numbers

25:6-13). Esther stood in the gap for her people, risking her life before the king (Esther 4:16). These weren't perfect people. They were willing.

Discipleship demands that kind of willingness. It's not about being fearless—it's about being faithful. I've flown missions where fear was thick in the cockpit. But I flew anyway. Because the mission mattered more than my fear of death, that's what following Christ feels like in this broken world. To stand between judgment and mercy. To intercede for those who can't. To speak truth when lies are popular. To love when hate is easier.

Isaiah 58:12 calls me to be a "repairer of the breach." That's not poetic—it's tactical. It means stepping into places where the enemy has gained ground and reclaiming them through prayer, service, and sacrifice. It means mentoring the next generation, confronting injustice, and living a life that reflects God's holiness.

The world doesn't need more spectators. I don't want to be a fan; I want to be a player. I want to be counted among those who will stand in the gap. Who says, "Here I am, Lord. Send me" (Isaiah 6:8). Not because I'm strong, but because He is. Not because I'm righteous but redeemed.

I've flown through storms. But the fiercest battles are spiritual. And in this ongoing cosmic war, discipleship means standing in the gap and flying in close formation with my flight leader, Jesus.

Jesus as a Fire Chief

When I first came to Christ, I was ablaze—lit with a fire that felt uncontainable. It was the kind of zeal that made every scripture shimmer, every prayer feel electric.

For nearly a decade, that fire burned brightly. But as time passed, I noticed the embers dimming. I tried to reignite what I thought I had lost, but the more I stoked, the more guilt I felt for the dwindling flame. I was reluctant to admit it to Jesus, which now seems naïve—He already knew the condition of my heart (Psalm 139:1–4).

Eventually, I found the courage to speak honestly with Him. In that

moment, Jesus gave me a vision—not of rebuke, but of reassurance. I saw Him as a fireman, one who had coordinated with the Father to provide me with the fire of the Holy Spirit (Luke 3:16). Then, He invited me to envision His promotion to Fire Chief, overseeing and leading Christian firefighters around the world.

As Fire Chief, His role isn't just to ignite but to equip. He trains us, deploys us, and sustains us. In my case, the fire hadn't gone out—it had been redirected. I asked Him, confused, "Why did You direct my fire away from You?"

His response was firm but loving. He reminded me of the words He spoke: "The greatest commandment is this: Love the Lord your God with all your heart, soul, and mind" (Matthew 22:37). To direct the full heat of your devotion toward the Father is not abandonment—it's alignment. Jesus, in His humility, always pointed toward the Father (John 14:28).

Then He told me the second part of His redirection was to use my fire not just for worship, but for service. To stoke flames of love in others, and to extinguish the destructive fires of doubt, anxiety, and anger. "Carry each other's burdens," Paul writes, "and in this way you will fulfill the law of Christ" (Galatians 6:2). Jesus reminded me that the fire within me is not mine to hoard—it's meant to be shared, stewarded, and sometimes even sacrificed for the sake of others.

Jesus reshaped how I see my walk. I'm not just a disciple—I'm a firefighter in His service. My gear is prayer, my water is grace, and the Spirit fuels my flame. And when I feel weary, I remember that the Fire Chief never leaves His crew behind. "He will not quench a smoldering wick" (Isaiah 42:3). He sees the flicker, fans it gently, and sends me back into the field ablaze.

So, I no longer fret about losing my fire but trust the One who lit it in the first place.

Shine as a Beacon of Light

Given my somewhat checkered past, I hardly see myself as anything close to being a beacon of light. The idea feels foreign—almost presumptuous. And yet, Paul's words in Philippians 2:15 leave little room for ambiguity: we are to "shine like lights in the world." Depending on the translation, it might say "stars in the universe," "bright lights," or "beacons." But the point remains—this isn't a flicker, a flashlight, or even a 100-watt bulb. It's a searchlight. A lighthouse. A radiant, unmistakable signal in the fog of a broken world. That's a tall order—one I could never generate on my own, nor even dare to try.

But Jesus never endorses a defeatist attitude. He is the Light of the world (John 8:12), and He draws that light from the source of all light—His Father—through the Holy Spirit, who now resides in me.

This spiritual wiring means I don't have to manufacture light; I need to flip the switch. The power is already there. Jesus doesn't merely suggest we shine—He commands it. In Matthew 5:14-16, He calls His disciples, like me, "the light of the world." More importantly, He urges me to shine my light before others so they may see my good works (empowered by the Holy Spirit) and glorify our Father in heaven. That's not optional. It's mission-critical.

Other Scriptures echo this call. Isaiah 60:1 says, "Arise, shine, for your light has come, and the glory of the Lord rises upon you." Ephesians 5:8 reminds us, "For at one time you were darkness, but now you are light in the Lord. Walk as children of light." And 1 Thessalonians 5:5 affirms, "You are all children of the light and children of the day. We do not belong to the night or to the darkness." These verses don't just describe a condition—they demand a posture. A way of living. A refusal to blend into the shadows.

But shining isn't just about visibility—it's about attitude. Paul precedes his call to shine with a challenge: "Do all things without grumbling or disputing" (Philippians 2:14). That's where the rubber meets the road. It's easy to shine when things are smooth. But when life gets gritty, when service feels thankless, when obedience costs something—that's when the light matters most. Joyful endurance, strength, and obedience become the wattage behind the witness.

And here's where I confess: I suffer from spiritual "switch-itis." I flick the light on when I feel inspired, and off when I feel inconvenienced. I shine when it suits me, and dim when it doesn't. But the call isn't to be a mood lamp—it's to be a lighthouse. Consistent. Unwavering. Positioned not for comfort, but for rescue. So, I return to my Source. I ask for grace not just to shine, but to stay lit. To resist the temptation to toggle based on my desires and instead live as one wired for divine illumination. Because the world doesn't need another flicker—it needs many beacons.

Life as in The Hereafter

As a tip-of-the-spear combatant, I've lived close to death—closer than most. I never enjoyed the killing, but I was good at it, especially when they were shooting back or in aerial combat. The U.S. government seemed to think I did my job well, as evidenced by the six Distinguished Flying Crosses and eleven Air Medals they awarded me. I honor these awards, but they don't compensate for the memories. Destruction leaves a residue that lingers. On Memorial Day, I mourn not only for my comrades who died honorably, but also for the enemy soldiers and their families—people whose lives were shattered by my combat missions during the Vietnam War.

Over the last five decades, Memorial Day has become a time of reflection for me. I think about death, yes—but more often, I think about what comes after. As a mature Christian, I concluded that there are four plausible options for life after death: none, temporary, eternal communion with God, and eternal separation from Him.

The first option—no life after death—is, in my view, a rational position for agnostics and atheists. It's also, I believe, an irrational hope for casual believers or cultural Christians. Except for the Zohar, the foundational work of Judaic Kabbalistic literature, and the Book of Enoch (which, though non-canonical, is quoted in Jude 1:14, 15), the idea of extinguishment doesn't hold much weight. The popular notion that death is like snuffing out a candle may comfort those who fear judgment, but if they're wrong, the consequences are eternal.

The second option is purgatory, a temporary suspension. Purgatory is an intermediate state where souls are purified before entering heaven. According to Catholic doctrine, it's for those who died in grace but still carry the residue of sin. I don't dismiss this view. It's a rational way to reconcile divine justice with mercy. But it's not final. It's a refining process, not a destination.

The final two options are eternal—heaven or hell. Entry is determined by judgment.

Those who turn toward the light of God while on earth will be welcomed into His kingdom. Those who chase material rewards will not. Scripture is clear on this. Ecclesiastes 8:15 and Isaiah 22:13 speak of those who seek merriment, "Let us eat and drink, for tomorrow we die." Jesus echoes this in Luke 12:19-21, warning against the folly of storing up earthly goods at the expense of the soul. For those who believe in an afterlife, I think pursuing worldly pleasures is a dangerous gamble. As for me, I choose Jesus—without hesitation.

For those who disagree, I remind them that God has granted humanity free will. In the end, I believe there are only two kinds of people: those who say to God, "Thy will be done," and those to whom God says, "Thy will be done." That's how I rationalize the unknowable. And that's how I live— with one eye on eternity, and both feet planted in Christ my Redeemer.

Centered as in the Center of the Bible

When I prayed for today's reflection, the word that came to me was  "center". I asked humbly, "Center of what?" but no further answer came. So I did what I usually do in that kind of silence— poured a cup of coffee, settled into my chair, and opened my devotional. The reading for the day was Psalm 118.

As I turned to the passage in my Bible, I noticed faded highlights and handwritten notes from nearly thirty years ago. I had once marked Psalm 118:8,9 as the exact center of the Bible by word count, a detail I had long forgotten. Seeing that note again felt like uncovering a reminder meant for this very moment. The verses read: "It is better to take refuge in the Lord than to trust in man. It is better to take refuge in the Lord than to trust in princes."

Those words carry weight. After decades in Washington, D.C., surrounded by government leaders and corporate executives, I have come to realize the limitations of human systems. Positions shift, policies change, and even the most powerful are fragile. Titles and institutions can only carry so much weight. Refuge must be found in something deeper, more enduring.

As I continued reading, the psalm opened up less like a set of verses and more like a framework for life. Verse 22 especially struck me: The stone the builders rejected has become the cornerstone. This is not just poetry—it is prophecy. Centuries before Christ, the psalmist pointed to the One whom Isaiah also foresaw eight hundred years earlier—the suffering servant, despised and rejected, who would become the foundation of salvation. What the builders cast aside, God used as the cornerstone of a kingdom that now spans the globe.

The psalm repeats, almost insistently, His steadfast love endures forever. The more I read it, the more it felt like an anchor. In today's upside-down transactional world, where spin wins, God's relationship does not change— at least not on His part. Then came the familiar line: "This is the day the Lord has made; let us rejoice and be glad in it." I've read those words countless times, but this time they felt personal. Other verses reminded me that God hears me in my distress, gives strength when mine runs out, and opens the narrow gate that leads to life in Christ.

After meditating on this Psalm, I understood what the Lord meant by "center." It wasn't just about word counting. It was about alignment. About anchoring. About placing my trust not in systems, titles, or institutions—but in Him. It was a gentle reminder to center my life on these revelations: refuge in the Lord, enduring love, divine design, and the narrow gate that leads to life. I don't claim to have all the answers. But I do know this: when the world feels off-kilter, Psalm 118 brings me back to the center.

Forgiveness as a Cultivated Habit

Forgiveness doesn't come naturally to me. I didn't grow up in an environment where grace was modeled or encouraged. My childhood was turbulent, marked by anger and a strong sense of survival. In my twenties, hardened by combat and the need to protect myself emotionally, I saw forgiveness as weakness. When I accepted Jesus Christ's invitation at age thirty, I found myself staring at a command I didn't know how to obey: forgive.

Letting go of resentment was more complicated than quitting smoking. And that's saying something—I wrestled with cigarettes for a decade before finally walking away. But bitterness? That lingered. It clung to me like smoke in my clothes, even when I thought I'd aired it out. The Holy Spirit, ever patient, reminds me that I'm a slow learner. Like an ex-smoker, I can backslide. Old habits don't die easily. But they can be replaced.

Forgiveness, I've learned, is not a one-time event. It's a process. Jesus' words in Matthew 18:22—"seventy times seven"—weren't poetic exaggeration. They were a prescription for someone like me. I forgive —and then forget that I've forgiven. I pick up old grudges like a football player losing four yards after gaining five. But I'm still moving forward. Inch by inch, with Jesus beside me and the Spirit within me, I strive for the goal line of the upward call.

Scripture doesn't mince words. It cajoles: "Forgive, as the Lord forgave you" (Colossians 3:13). And it warns: "If you do not forgive others their sins, your Father will not forgive your sins" (Matthew 6:15). That contrast sobers me. It's not just about being a good person—it's about living in alignment with the mercy I've received.

The Lord's Prayer, in its Protestant form, is only fifty words long. Yet forgive appears twice. That repetition isn't accidental. When I pray it, I

personalize the plea: "Forgive me my many trespasses in thought, word, and deed, as I forgive those who trespass against me—intentionally, unintentionally, and even in my perception only." Most days, my own failings far outweigh the wrongs done to me. That perspective keeps me grounded.

Over time, I've come to see forgiveness and resentment as two sides of the same coin—just like love and hate. Forgiveness lifts. It releases me from the weight of anger and the impulse for retaliation. Resentment corrodes. It eats away at body and soul.

I see forgiveness as a habit I must cultivate. It's spiritual muscle memory maintained not by my willpower, but by the will of God, the example of Jesus, and the power of the Holy Spirit. It's part of the trek on the twisting path towards the narrow gate.

Jesus as Living Water

I have been reflecting on Jesus as living water and on how the Holy Spirit purifies what He provides for me, enabling me to lead an abundant and healthy life. That reflection has drawn me back to my years in high-tech water business initiatives—developing systems that transform polluted water into clean, drinkable sources of life. I've always seen clean water as a sacred provision.

In John 4, Jesus meets a Samaritan woman at Jacob's well. She comes for  physical water, but He offers something far more profound: "Whoever drinks the water I give them will never thirst. Indeed, the water I give them will become in them a spring of water welling up to eternal life" (John 4:14). That moment wasn't just about revelation—it was about restoration. Jesus didn't shame her history; He invited her into renewal. And the agent of that renewal, the living water, is the Holy Spirit.

Just as polluted water must pass through membranes, filters, and UV light to be made clean, our hearts—clouded by pride, pain, and distortion— require the Spirit's refining presence, not in a mystical or overly spiritualized way, but in the quiet, daily work of conviction, comfort, and clarity. The Spirit doesn't just cleanse; He restores us to the purity God intended.

In Ezekiel 36:25–27, God promises, "I will sprinkle clean water on you, and you will be clean... I will give you a new heart and put a new spirit in you." That passage echoes the same theme: purification precedes transformation. And in Isaiah 12:3, we're told, "With joy you will draw water from the wells of salvation." Again, the metaphor is not abstract—it's tangible. Water is essential, and so is the Spirit's work in making us whole.

I've seen firsthand how contaminated water can be made safe to drink again. It takes intentional design, rigorous testing, and constant flow. Likewise, the Spirit's purification isn't a one-time event. It's a process—ongoing, iterative, and deeply personal. He doesn't just remove the obvious toxins; He reaches into the hidden places, the sediment of our stories, and filters them through grace.

The woman at the well left her jar behind. That detail matters. She came for water, but she found something better. And in doing so, she became a vessel herself—carrying the news of living water to her village. That's the invitation for me, too. Not to be perfect, but to be purified. Not to be the source, but to be a vessel through which the Spirit flows. And in that vesselhood, I've found that the Holy Spirit continually refreshes me with the living water that Jesus provides—cleansing, sustaining, and renewing me day by day.

Discipline as in Weary of His Reproof

"My son, do not despise the Lord's discipline or be weary of his reproof." Proverbs 3:11 (RSV)

There was a time when I mistook the Lord's correction for distance. I felt wearied by His reproof, as if it were a sign of disfavor rather than love. But the longer I walk with Him, the more I see that His discipline is not a withdrawal but shaping me into a vessel fit for His glory. Scripture affirms this truth repeatedly. Hebrews 12:6 declares, "For the Lord disciplines him whom he loves, and chastises every son whom he receives." This is the tenderness of a Father who sees what I cannot. His reproof is not punishment for failure, but preparation for faithfulness.

I've come to understand that discipline is the doorway to usefulness. "All scripture is inspired by God and profitable for teaching, for reproof, for correction, and for training in righteousness, that the man of God may be complete, equipped for every good work" (2 Tim 3:16). I once longed to be used by God without being refined by Him. Now I see that the refining is the very process that equips me to do good works in Jesus, according to His will and purpose.

God's reproof is not random—it is precise. Revelation 3:19 says, "Those whom I love, I reprove and chasten; so be zealous and repent." His correction is not condemnation—it is an invitation. An invitation to turn, to trust, to be transformed.

And though the process is painful, the fruit is peace. Hebrews 12:11 speaks plainly: "For the moment all discipline seems painful rather than pleasant; later it yields the peaceful fruit of righteousness to those who have been

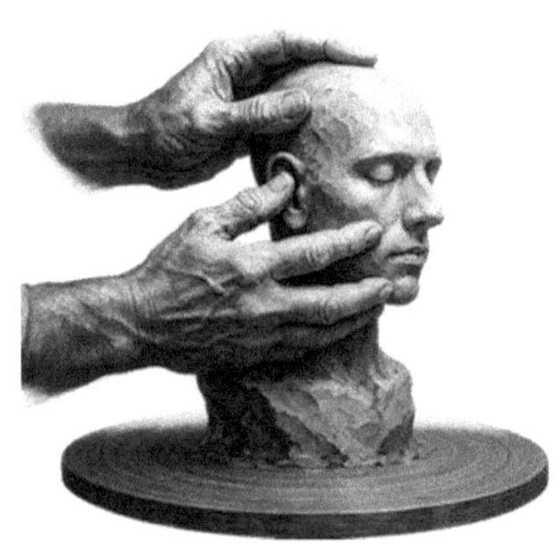

trained by it." I've tasted that fruit—not the sweetness of ease, but the depth of peace that comes from knowing I am aligned with His purpose.

Ephesians 2:10 tells me that "we are his workmanship, created in Christ Jesus for good works, which God prepared beforehand, that we should walk in them." But I cannot walk in those works unless I first submit to His workmanship. The molding and remolding of the great Potter, the humbling, and the reproof are all part of becoming the kind of person who reflects Jesus rather than resists Him, and a vessel for good works.

So yes, I have grown weary of His reproof. But I now see weariness as a sign of my resistance, not a rejection by Him. And I am learning to surrender—not out of defeat, but out of desire to be made whole.

Ironically, I believe that I can be the person that God created me to be if I decrease and let Jesus increase in me. By doing so, rather than losing my identity, He will unveil my true identity that a worldly orientation and its influence have shrouded.

Loyalty and Faithfulness as Not Forsaken

"Let not loyalty and faithfulness forsake you; bind them about your neck, write them on the tablet of your heart." Proverbs 3:3 (RSV)

There was a time when loyalty felt conditional to me—something I offered when it was reciprocated, something I withheld when it cost too much. Faithfulness, too, seemed easier to profess than to practice. But the Lord, in His quiet persistence, began to show me that these are not virtues to be worn when convenient. They are to be written on the tablet of my heart.

I've come to see that loyalty and faithfulness are not just moral ideals. They are reflections of God's own nature. Exodus 34:6 describes Him as "abounding in steadfast love and faithfulness." If I am to bear His image, these traits must not merely visit me—they must dwell in me.

When I let loyalty and faithfulness slip, I drift from the character of Christ. Micah 6:8 reminds me that the Lord requires me "to do justice, and to love kindness, and to walk humbly with [my] God." That kindness is the very root of loyalty and faithfulness. They are not seasonal. They are steadfast. And I am learning that they must be visible in me, not just professed by me. They must shape my speech, my decisions, my relationships. They must be written not in ink, but in obedience.

Faithfulness is not proven in moments of ease, but in seasons of testing. Luke 16:10 says, "He who is faithful in a very little is faithful also in much." I've come to believe that the Lord watches how I handle the quiet commitments—the ones no one sees. These are the places where loyalty is forged. And when I fail—and I do—I return to the One who never forsakes me. 2 Timothy 2:13 comforts me: "If we are faithless, He remains faithful—for He cannot deny Himself." His loyalty is not reactive—it is rooted in His nature.

I've come to believe that loyalty and faithfulness are not burdens, but blessings. They are the scaffolding upon which the Spirit builds a life that reflects Jesus. They are the evidence that I am being transformed—not conformed. The more I surrender myself to the will of God, the more Christ is revealed through me.

As John the Baptist declared, "He must increase, but I must decrease" (John 3:30). This isn't self-erasure—it's spiritual unveiling. It's kenosis, or voluntary self-emptying, as Christ demonstrated while He was on earth.

When I step back from the spotlight of self, I reflect the radiance and face of Jesus. And in that light, I don't vanish—I emerge. Not as the version shaped by worldly expectations, but as the true self God intended: refined, restored, and rooted in Him as a loyal and faithful disciple.

God as the Divine Accountant

There are moments when I wonder if God notices what I'm doing. I pray and hear no answer. I step out in faith, only to meet silence. I've made decisions prompted by the Holy Spirit's nudge that led seemingly nowhere. And in those moments, discouragement settles in like fog.

Over time, I've come to understand that I'm not alone in this feeling. Even Jesus experienced the ache of being dismissed and overlooked. He healed the sick and raised the dead, yet many refused to believe. He preached truth, yet the religious leaders scorned Him. He poured into His disciples, only to be abandoned in His hour of greatest need. If anyone knows what it feels like to give everything and not be fully received, it is Jesus. Yet, He kept going.

Why? Because He trusted the Father's will, wisdom, and watchfulness.

That watchfulness is not passive. Malachi 3:16 reveals a striking truth: "Then those who feared the Lord spoke with one another, and the Lord listened and heard them. So, a scroll of remembrance was written before Him for those who feared the Lord and honored His name." God keeps a record of our reverence, our motives, our unseen obedience. He is not indifferent. He is the Divine Accountant, meticulously recording every act of faithfulness.

This truth echoes in Matthew 25:31-46, where Jesus separates the righteous from the unrighteous. The righteous are stunned: "Lord, when did we see You hungry and feed You?" They hadn't kept track—but He had. "Whatever you did for one of the least of these brothers and sisters of Mine, you did for Me." Acts they had forgotten, God had faithfully recorded.

Paul affirms this divine accounting: "Therefore, my dear brothers and sisters, be steadfast, immovable, always abounding in the work of the Lord, because you know that your labor in the Lord is not in vain." (1 Corinthians 15:58) That assurance means more to me with each passing year.

This image of God as the Divine Accountant changes how I respond to discouragement. Just because I don't see the results doesn't mean my faithfulness is wasted. Earthly outcomes don't measure heaven's ledger. He sees the motive. He counts the cost. And He remembers.

So, I keep showing up. Even when my prayers seem unanswered, even when the world overlooks the effort, even when I wonder if anything will come of it, I trust that God is paying attention. He's not just watching—He's recording.

On Judgment Day, I'll witness the record of my life, both good and bad. In that moment, I'll know that not one iota of my faith, love, or obedience was forgotten. In Jesus, covered by His sacrifice for me, the only things forgotten will be my sinful acts, deeds, words, and thoughts.

Holy Spirit as My Superpower

When Jesus came to Earth, He willingly set aside His royal privileges, prestige, and divine powers—retaining only one: the Holy Spirit. In doing so, Jesus became fully human, living as we do, yet demonstrating the limitless superpower of the Holy Spirit at work in Him.

Jesus modeled complete reliance on God's Spirit, teaching His disciples—then and now—how to access this same divine power. Throughout His ministry, He performed extraordinary miracles, not through personal ability, but by the guidance and power of the Holy Spirit. When He raised Lazarus from the dead (John 11:41-44), Jesus first lifted His eyes to heaven, thanking His Father before calling Lazarus forth. At His baptism, the Holy Spirit descended upon Him like a dove (Luke 3:22), marking the beginning of His public ministry. He healed the sick, restored sight to the blind, and calmed the raging sea—all through divine empowerment.

On the day of Pentecost (Acts 2), Jesus fulfilled His promise by bestowing the Holy Spirit upon His disciples, equipping them with the same power He had relied upon during His time on Earth. This wasn't a symbolic gesture—it was a transfer of divine capability.

As a disciple of Jesus, I have access to this incredible power—the Spirit of God who dwells within me, transforming me daily into a vessel of good works, producing the aroma of Christ and the fruits of the Spirit (Galatians 5:22-23), which pleases God the Father. Yet, even after years of walking in faith, I continue to learn how to access this divine superpower. In many ways, I am like a child learning to ride a bike with training wheels—sometimes steady, sometimes stumbling, but always inching forward, albeit wobbly.

My biggest challenge in accessing the Spirit's power is quieting myself, just as Jesus did before many of His miracles. Scripture tells us that the Spirit speaks with a "still small voice" (1 Kings 19:12), as Elijah experienced on Mount Horeb. The Spirit's gentle whisper remains constant, but the noise of this world competes for my attention. Satan and his forces attempt to disrupt my connection, increasing the volume of distractions that try to drown the Spirit's subdued tone.

I find myself frustrated with the Holy Spirit for not simply talking louder to mitigate the clamor. But that frustration reveals my misunderstanding: the Spirit does not shout over chaos; He invites me to step into stillness. Jesus demonstrated this level of concentration.

Unlike Marvel superheroes with flashy abilities, the Holy Spirit's power is activated not by personal strength but by surrender. As I continue on this journey, I will strive to listen more closely, quiet the noise, and allow the Spirit to work through me—not for my glory, but for God.

Prayer as a Dialogue

Over the years, I've come to see prayer not as ritual, but as a relationship—a dialogue with God. Scripture urges me to seek Him, so I did. At first, I leaned on familiar prayers—the Lord's Prayer, "Bless the Lord, O my soul," blessings over meals. They sustained me for a time. But eventually, they felt hollow, mechanical. Then one day, to my surprise, God spoke back.

He told me He wanted a dialogue, not a sacrifice of time or contrite words. I asked, "Who are you, Lord? Who am I speaking to?" He answered, "I am Jesus, but I am also Holy Spirit and Father; We are One." I asked, "How can I address you?" He said, "Let your spirit communicate with my Spirit, and We will intercede on your behalf with the Father."

That moment reshaped my understanding of prayer. It wasn't about presenting needs or reciting phrases—it was about engaging in a living conversation. Scripture affirms that God speaks back, inviting us into deeper communion. I've heard His voice through the Word, through my heart, through others, and at times, through direct revelation.

First, God speaks through scripture. The Bible is not static—it's alive. Hebrews 4:12 says, "The word of God is living and active, sharper than any two-edged sword." Often, verses leap off the page, addressing my questions with startling clarity. Psalm 119:105 affirms, "Your word is a lamp to my feet and a light to my path." Time and again, scripture illuminates my steps.

God also speaks to my heart. John 10:27 says, "My sheep hear my voice, and I know them, and they follow me." I've felt this as quiet conviction or peace in decision-making—an inner compass aligning me with His will. Luke 24:32 echoes this: "Did not our hearts burn within us while He talked to us on the road?" These moments, though subtle, are fantastic.

God also speaks through others. In scripture, He used prophets; today, He uses friends, pastors, and even strangers. Hebrews 1:1 reminds us, "Long ago, at many times and in many ways, God spoke to our fathers by the prophets." 2 Peter 1:21 adds, "Men spoke from God as the Holy Spirit carried them along." I've received timely words from others that felt divinely orchestrated.

Occasionally, God speaks through revelation. Jeremiah 33:3 says, "Call to me and I will answer you, and will tell you great and hidden things." Revelation 1:1 speaks of God unveiling truths to His servants. I've had insights that felt divinely given—aligned with scripture and circumstance. I don't chase them; they come as He wills.

Prayer, as a dialogue, has become a lifeline. It's not about perfect words, but an honest exchange. I know this to be true because when we talk, the Father often calls me "child," the Holy Spirit addresses me as "blessed," and my Savior Jesus occasionally refers to me as "friend."

Agape as Beyond Self

Most Christians are familiar with the three Greek expressions of love: eros (romantic), philia (brotherly), and agape—the latter often described as selfless, unconditional, and sacrificial. But for me, agape didn't start as a divine ideal. It began as a transaction.

When I first came to Christ, I understood agape through the Golden Rule (Matthew 7:12): "Do unto others as you would have them do unto you." It felt fair, logical—like a moral handshake. But it was still about me. I loved others because I wanted to be loved back. That's not agape. That's just insurance. As I grew in faith, Jesus' Great Commandment raised the stakes (Matthew 22:37-39): "Love your neighbor as yourself." That sounded noble, but also exhausting. Fortunately, Jesus didn't expect me to do it alone. Through the Holy Spirit, I learned to access the source of all love— His Father. Still, I resisted. I liked control. I liked knowing the terms.

Then Jesus raised the bar again: "Love one another as I have loved you." (John 15:12). He blessed enemies. He laid down His life. I felt the weight of that call, and I flinched. That's when He gave me a vision, a daydream, as His wingman, flying in formation. Jesus lit the afterburners of His F-4 Phantom II and zoom climbed upward. I followed, barely keeping pace.

Then came the radio call: "Accept the reproaches of those who reproached others to fall on thee." (Romans 15:3). "What?" I muttered, watching my air speed rapidly bleeding off. "Lord, can we talk about this later when we're on the ground?" He laughed and climbed higher. Then came another call: "Bless those who persecute you." I asked Him to repeat it. He did. I muttered, "Roger." I was starting to wonder about my flight leader. I started sweating. And then—He inverted. Dove straight down toward Earth. I tucked in close, heart pounding. "There is no greater love than to lay down your life for others." (John 15:13). I froze. "Say again?" Silence.

Seeing the ground rushing up in my peripheral vision, I faced a critical decision—stay in formation or break away from this madman. The Holy Spirit whispered, "Stay with Him." As soon as I did, Jesus abruptly yanked the nose of His jet upward into a nine-G pullout. I held on—barely. I wet

myself under the pressure, bracing for impact. I was terrified. But I didn't let go. As we leveled out at tree-top altitude, He laughingly radioed: "Now that's what I call AGAPE!"

Safely on the ground, Jesus explained that true agape is beyond self. It's not a transaction—it's surrender. Our Father surrendered My life for you. Abraham was willing to sacrifice his son because he loved God beyond himself. You stayed on My wing during that perilous dive, trusting My leadership when the world would have done otherwise. That is what I mean by agape. And with that bit of wisdom, He concluded my Agape daydream.

Trust as a Trapeze

In today's transactional world—where every interaction feels like a calculated exchange, whether in business deals, social media likes, or even friendships—trust doesn't come easily to me. I've been burned too many times by broken promises and hidden agendas. So I became guarded, weighing risks before extending even a sliver of vulnerability.

When I first became a Christian, trusting God felt like a risky venture. Here was the Omnipotent God asking for my whole heart, my unreserved faith, and I was riddled with doubts. Worse still, Scripture seemed to condemn people like me. James 1:6-8 describes the doubter as a wave tossed by the wind, double-minded and unstable, receiving nothing from the Lord.

Taking that initial leap of faith felt like trusting daring trapeze acrobats who perform high above the ground without a net. That's how trusting God felt: a gamble, one misstep away from disaster. My mind raced with "what ifs," much like Peter in Matthew 14:31, who walked on water toward Jesus but sank when fear overtook him. Jesus' rebuke, "O you of little faith, why did you doubt?" resonated, but it also stung, exposing my faltering faith and trust.

Over time, I learned that overcoming doubt isn't a single, death-defying leap. It's a gradual process—a series of small trusts built over time. The Bible doesn't demand instant perfection; it invites a journey. Proverbs 3:5-6 urges,

"Trust in the Lord with all your heart, and do not lean on your own understanding." It acknowledges our human tendency to overthink. Trust isn't about erasing doubt overnight—it's about accepting God in all things and letting Him straighten our paths, step by step.

Jesus modeled patience with doubters like me. In John 20:27-29, He didn't scold Thomas for needing proof of the resurrection. He invited him to touch His wounds. That same compassion echoes in Mark 11:22-23, where Jesus teaches that faith without doubt can move mountains—but He pairs it with encouragement, knowing that growth comes through practice.

Psalm 42:5-6 became my mantra in contemplative moments: "Why are you cast down, O my soul? Hope in God." It's a self-dialogue—honest about inner turmoil yet redirecting toward trust. Through prayer, community, and Scripture, my doubts began to soften. Not vanished—life's winds still buffet—but transformed into deeper reliance, like Isaiah 26:3-4 promises: perfect peace for the mind stayed on Him.

Today, I no longer see trust as a reckless leap into the unknown. I see it as a practiced rhythm between the flyer and the Catcher. My role is not to perform flawlessly, but to release at the right moment and reach toward the One who never misses. The trapeze is still high, the fall still real, but the Catcher is faithful.

God as Not an Option

I've treated God like an option more times than I care to admit. I never doubted His sovereignty, but in the way I made life choices. I planned, built, and even prayed as if He were a supporting actor in my story rather than the Author. It's subtle, but it shows. And when I slow down long enough to reflect, I realize how inverted that posture really is.

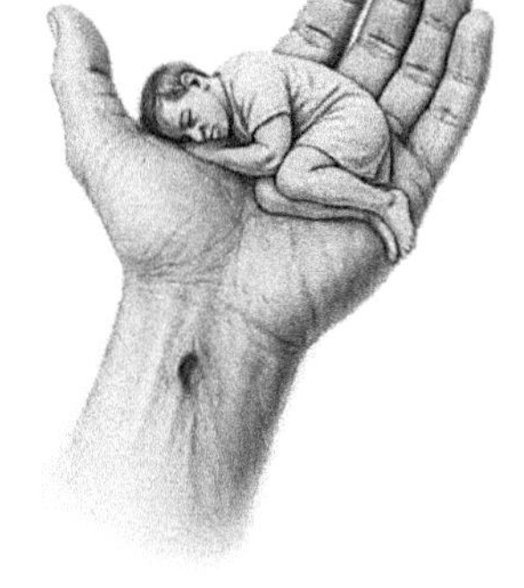

He is eternal. I am dust. I was formed from the ground, and I'll return to it. He, on the other hand, formed the ground itself. "All things were created through Him and for Him," Paul writes in Colossians 1:16. That includes me. I'm not the center. I am His creation, sustained moment by moment by His will. He holds me in the palm of His hand. He is significant. He gives me purpose and meaning.

And still, I drift. I start to believe I'm the one holding things together. I treat God like someone to call in when the gears grind or the path gets foggy. Scripture doesn't support that kind of casualness. In Acts 17:28, Paul reminds the Athenians, "In Him we live and move and have our being." That's not metaphor—it's reality. I don't just believe in Him. I exist in Him.

Revelation 4 gives a glimpse of how heaven responds to that truth. The elders fall before His throne, casting their crowns and declaring, "Worthy are You, our Lord and God... for You created all things." There's no presumption in their worship—only clarity. They know who He is. They know who they are. The noncanonical Book of Enoch offers an even deeper glimpse into that reverence. Even the archangels, radiant and mighty, approach His throne with trembling awe. Not fear born of punishment, but of purity—an awareness of His majesty that strips away presumption. If they, who dwell in His presence, bow low, how much more should I?

I've had moments like that. Not dramatic ones, but quiet realizations—usually when something I built starts to crack. A job plan unravels. A relationship fails. An ambition proves hollow. And in those moments, I remember that every breath is borrowed. Every opportunity to know Him is grace. And I wonder how many times I've mistaken His patience for passivity, as if His silence meant indifference rather than mercy.

Hebrews 10:31 says, "It is a fearful thing to fall into the hands of the living God." That used to unsettle me. Now it sobers me. Not because I doubt His mercy, but because I'm learning to respect His holiness. He's not optional. He's not peripheral. He's the center, whether I acknowledge Him or not.

So I remind myself often: God doesn't orbit my life. I orbit His. When I forget that, I shrink Him down to something manageable. But He's not manageable. He's magnificent. He is not an option to weigh—He is the One in whom all things hold together. And I am dust. Loved dust—held together by grace—but dust, nonetheless.

Blasphemy as the Unforgivable Sin

There are passages in Scripture that don't just speak—they confront. Jesus'  words about blasphemy against the Holy Spirit are among them. This passage is much more than a warning. It reads like a final verdict—an irreversible death sentence.

"Every sin and blasphemy will be forgiven people, but blasphemy against the Spirit will not be forgiven..." (Matthew 12:31). Mark calls it an eternal sin. Hebrews 10 warns of "outraging the Spirit of grace." Hebrews 6 describes those who once tasted the goodness of God yet fell away—and of them it says, "it is impossible to restore them to repentance." The penalty of an unrepentant soul is eternal separation from God, described biblically as death, the second death, or banishment to the lake of fire. It's the finality that unnerves me.

The principalities and powers that rule this world are committed to hardening a person's heart so profoundly that they will no longer want grace at all. That's the real danger—not that forgiveness has a limit, but that I could conceivably reject the One who offers it.

The Holy Spirit is not a passive observer. He's the one who convicts, comforts, and draws me toward truth. He doesn't shout—but I know when

He's nudging. And that's what makes Jesus' strong admonition so heavy: to blaspheme the Spirit is not a single act of ignorance or doubt, but a clear-eyed rejection of His testimony about Christ. It's choosing darkness after seeing light. Not stumbling—it's turning and walking away.

I used to think this vehement caution was meant for "them"—people far from God, hardened skeptics, mockers. But lately I've wondered if the real danger is subtler. I can become familiar with the Spirit's voice and start tuning it out. I can acknowledge the truth but still delay obedience. I can mask resistance with busyness or bury conviction beneath noise. That scares me more than outright defiance.

There's a strange echo in Genesis. Adam and Eve took one bite, and it was enough to lose the garden—a single act, but one that severed trust. Blasphemy of the Spirit seems like its mirror image: not a bite, but a final refusal of the remedy. One act closes Eden's gates; the other keeps heaven's gates permanently shut.

I'm writing this Analogy because I need to hear it. These are not verses to dissect but to internalize. And maybe the most honest thing I can say is this: I don't want to flirt with the edge of what God calls unforgivable. I want to notice when my heart starts to drift and respond without delay when the Spirit whispers—before resistance hardens into indifference. If procrastination becomes a habit, I want to interrupt it—not with guilt, but with resolve.

Once Saved as Always Saved

When I first came to Christ, I clung tightly to Romans 8:38-39: "Nothing can separate us from the love of God that is in Christ Jesus our Lord." That verse was a lifeline. It told me that no matter what I faced—no principality, no power, no failure—His love would hold me fast. And from that, I drew a conclusion that many new believers do: "once saved, always saved."

It was comforting. It gave me peace. But over time, as I grew in faith and began to read Scripture with more context and less assumption, I started to notice verses that didn't fit so neatly into that framework. They didn't contradict God's love—but they did challenge my understanding of what it means to abide in Him.

Jesus' warning about blasphemy against the Holy Spirit was the first jolt. "It will not be forgiven," He said (Matthew 12:31). That didn't sound like a blanket guarantee. Then came the parables, stories I had once skimmed over but now couldn't ignore.

In Matthew 25, all ten bridesmaids believed in the groom. They were waiting with lit candles for Him. But only five were ready when He arrived. The others were locked out.

In the same chapter, the servant who buried his talent wasn't praised for playing it safe—he was cast into outer darkness. And the parable of the sower reminded me that some receive the word with joy but fall away when trouble comes or when the cares of life choke the seed. These weren't stories about unbelievers. They were about people who started well but didn't endure and were cast out from the presence of their Lord.

The most sobering image, though, is the sheep and the goats. Both groups refer to Jesus as "Lord." But to the goats, He says, "I never knew you." That line still unsettles me. It suggests that proximity to Jesus—familiarity with His name—isn't the same as intimacy with Him.

So I've had to reevaluate. Not because I doubt God's faithfulness, but because I've come to see how fragile my own can be. Salvation is a gift, yes. But it's also a relationship. And like any relationship, it requires presence, trust, and response. I don't believe Jesus ever lets go of those who are truly His. But I do believe it's possible to walk so far away that we no longer hear His voice—or worse, no longer want to.

This isn't about fear. It's about focus. Following Jesus isn't a one-time decision—it's a daily one. And while His love never fails, I've learned that mine can. Not because He broke the bond, but because I did. So I keep watch. I tend the oil. I invest what He's given. Not to earn salvation, but to honor it. Because grace is free—but it was never meant to be taken for granted.

Blessed as in Poor in Spirit

As an agnostic, when I first heard the phrase "Blessed are the poor in spirit," I dismissed it outright. It sounded like religious gibberish—a cryptic koan more fitting for a cult than any congregation that claimed a semblance of reason. The phrase struck me as intentionally confusing, almost manipulative in its paradox. Why would anyone celebrate spiritual emptiness?

As a fledgling Christian, my perspective changed—but only slightly. The Beatitudes in Matthew 5:3-10 felt like a spiritual Rubik's cube: full of color and promise, yet frustratingly unsolvable. I gave up quickly, tossing the whole passage aside along with my initial momentum of faith. It seemed easier to chase clarity elsewhere than wrestle with riddles that refused to yield.

Later, as a follower of Jesus still wrestling to grasp His teachings, I tried to flip the script. I thought maybe Jesus was inverting everything—maybe "blessed" really meant "cursed," and vice versa. I began to view spiritually poor as the opposite of the humanly prideful, concluding that those who cling to pride are cursed, while those who empty themselves are blessed. It was an improvement in understanding, but still only surface-level. Something deeper was stirring beneath those words.

Now, as a disciple learning the rhythm of surrender, I'm beginning to understand that being poor in spirit isn't about weakness or confusion—it's about openness. It's about living with empty hands and a surrendered will. It's the posture of one who knows that every ounce of goodness is received, not produced. True blessedness begins when self-sufficiency ends.

Looking back, it reminds me of the parable of the Sower. The Word fell on different hearts—each one representing a stage in my own faith journey. The agnostic heart quickly lost the seed, snatched away by skepticism. As a new believer, the Word sprouted but found no depth—withered by spiritual impatience and shallow soil. As a follower entangled in life's distractions, the seed was choked out by worry, ambition, and ego. But slowly, by grace, the soil of my heart deepened. And the deeper the roots, the greater the harvest.

I want to say I'm producing thirty-, sixty-, or a hundred-fold. On a good day, maybe twenty. On others, thorns creep in, or the soil lies unattended. But I'm learning: the measure of my fruitfulness isn't found in performance, but in surrender. God does not call me to be impressive—He calls me to be available.

So yes, blessed as in poor in spirit. Not as pitiful, but as prepared. Emptied of self, ready to be filled. Blessed are those who come to the end of themselves—not in despair, but in divine dependence. Because in that empty space, grace takes root and grows best.

A Mute as a Storyteller

"The heavens declare the glory of God; the skies proclaim the work of his hands. Day after day, they pour forth their speech; night after night, they reveal their knowledge. They have no speech; they use no words; no sound is heard from them."
— Psalm 19:1-3 NIV

It amazes me how the most profound truths aren't always shouted—they're

often whispered or not spoken at all. When I pause long enough to look up—really look—I notice that the sky is never silent. Sunrise and sunset paint the gospel across the heavens in colors no human voice could compose. Stars blink with unspoken testimony. Everything in creation is telling His story—a mute storyteller with a voice that somehow fills the earth.

But I confess: I don't always hear it. For every whisper from above, the world offers a thousand clamors below. Screens blink. Newsfeeds scroll—influencers, leaders, pundits—each one clamoring for attention. Even my own thoughts betray me at times, rehearsing worries and chasing vanities. I try to tune into the divine frequency, but the static of life overwhelms me. My struggle is not one of belief, but of bandwidth. I've got a signal-to-noise ratio problem. The more intently I try to hear from God, the louder the enemy dials up the distractions.

The words of Psalm 19 strike me with humble irony: "They have no speech...yet their voice goes out." God's message isn't bound to syllables. His creation speaks in resonance rather than rhetoric. But that kind of language requires a different type of hearing. It requires stillness. It requires surrender. And that's where I fall short—often and honestly.

Sometimes I imagine myself as a radio with a bent antenna, desperately rotating to catch the right station. I might tune in for a moment, hearing divine harmony, but then a commercial from the world interrupts: You're not enough. You need more. You're missing out. Just like that, the story of God's glory is drowned out by marketing schemes and counterfeit kingdoms.

But here's the hope: I am not alone in the listening. The Holy Spirit is my signal booster. When I rely on my own strength, the message becomes distorted. But when I surrender, the Spirit clarifies. He speaks without sound and guides without noise. It is His voice that helps me discern God's voice—in the rustle of trees, in the ache of my own soul, in the silence of a starry night.

Yet like any skill, this kind of hearing must be honed—daily and deliberately. Without practice, the world's volume creeps back in. The mute storyteller keeps speaking, but I grow deaf. So each day, I quiet myself again. I open the windows of my heart and let the heavens speak. The story hasn't changed— but I'm learning how to listen. And when I do, I don't just hear—I understand.

Heaven as a Homecoming

Sometimes I think life here is a little like boot camp, unpredictable, demanding, and at times, downright confusing. But at the core of it all, I've come to believe it's a test, like a proving ground—a place where faith, character, and love are refined—a journey with purpose.

For me, that purpose points homeward. And by "home," I don't mean the house I grew up in, or even the memories that make me nostalgic. I mean heaven—my real home. The place where I belong is not because I earned it, but because Jesus opened the gate. Where my Master and Savior wait with open arms, ready to welcome a weary traveler when this brief chapter of life ends.

There's something about the word "home" that quiets the noise. A place of rest after the road, belonging after wandering, peace after struggle. That image lines up with what Jesus said when He promised to prepare a place for those who follow Him (John 14:2-3). To me, that sounds like a personal assurance: "I haven't forgotten you. I know what you long for. I'll be there when you arrive."

But the journey itself? It's not easy. This world offers plenty of diversions—some pleasant, some painful—and they can all blur the destination if I'm not careful. I've stumbled more than once. I've taken detours and wasted time chasing what doesn't last. But when I come back to what matters, I remember: I'm not just surviving here. I'm training for something greater.

Scripture says our time here is like a race or a trial (2 Timothy 4:7, James 1:12). It's not about perfection—it's about perseverance. And when the final exam is over, so to speak, the passing grade isn't based on my performance but on my trust in the One who gave everything to get me home.

I take comfort in Paul's reminder that we're citizens of heaven (Philippians 3:20). That means this world is not my final address. It's a temporary post. And as beautiful as some days can be, they're just a glimpse of the place I was made for.

I'm not in a hurry to leave this life, but I'm also not clinging to it. When the time comes, I hope to arrive at heaven like someone returning from deployment—worn, maybe, but not empty, with stories, lessons, and a spirit that, by grace, reflects a bit of the One who sent me.

And when I finally stand at that threshold—past the striving, past the noise—I pray I hear the words that matter more than any other: Well done. Welcome home. Join me. (Matthew 25:23)

The End as The Beginning

Jesus said, "I am with you always, even to the end of the age" (Matthew 28:20). That word—always—used to puzzle me. It felt so permanent, like a promise outside of time. But then He added "to the end of the age," and suddenly it sounded like a countdown. It took me a while to realize that maybe the end of the age isn't a termination point, but a transition. Perhaps it's not a closing scene—but the beginning of the next act.

Over time, I've come to think of this life as a test, yes, but not an exam. It's a refining process in which those who seek God begin to sense His rhythm. For those who deny Him or prefer the noise of the world, there may be another path they follow, one of separation. But for those who walk with Jesus, the end of this age feels less like leaving and more like arriving.

Scripture tells us that one day God will usher in a new heaven and a new earth (Revelation 21:1). The old world will pass, and something entirely new will take its place. I can't imagine it fully, but I do picture a reality untouched by death, grief, or deceit. And somewhere within that reality, I believe I'll be reunited with Christ—not as a figure seen through the lens of history, but as the very embodiment of truth and love.

The first lines of the Gospel of John say something that has always left me in awe: In the beginning was the Word, and the Word was with God, and the Word was God (John 1:1-2). That's Jesus—there before time, one with the Father, and through Him all things came into being. I'm no theologian, but I sometimes wonder if Jesus was a manifestation of God's essence—a form created to be seen and touched by creation. And perhaps when this spiritual era concludes, He returns to the Father in perfect unity, bringing with Him the souls He redeemed. A great gathering. A return to source.

Now, I know that may not be a textbook explanation. I might be way off. But in my spirit, I sense joy from the Lord when I ponder such things—not because I've got the mechanics right, but because I'm looking toward Him at all. The Holy Spirit seems to nudge me, saying, "Keep wondering. Keep seeking. Your questions are music to the Father's ears—even if they're out of tune."

So if the end of the age is truly a beginning, then I have nothing to fear. Because the same Jesus who was with us in the beginning, the same One who walks beside us now, will still be with us—just in a fullness we can't yet comprehend.

Maybe that's what "always" really means. Not a mark on the timeline—but a presence, infinite and undivided, from start to forever.

Soaring as on Spiritual Winds

Isaiah 40:31 has long spoken to something deep in my spirit.

Isaiah's image of soaring on wings like eagles, running and not growing weary—it's a promise that has taken on different shades of meaning over time. In my earlier days, I experienced something few ever do: literal flight, high and fast in supersonic jets. For hours at a time, I moved above the earth in mechanical birds, machines that made the eagle's metaphor feel real. But always, the flight was temporary. The fuel gauge dictated the limits. Eventually, gravity pulled me back to the runway.

These days, I'm no longer strapped into a cockpit. A quieter search for lift has replaced the roar of afterburners. Now, I'm learning to soar differently—one far less dependent on engines and altitude, and far more dependent on trust. The wind beneath me is no longer generated by turbines but sustained by God's uplifting Spirit.

This isn't an effortless flight. If anything, it reminds me more of a fledgling bird learning to trust its wings. My attempts can feel frantic, even clumsy. In the absence of confidence, instinct sometimes takes over, and I flap harder than I need to, forgetting that what I truly need is to rest into the wind.

Something is humbling in that image of effortless flight. The Spirit is constant, moving like wind across the surface of our lives, ready to lift any soul willing to ride its current. But like Peter stepping onto the water, I'm easily distracted. My eyes wander. Doubt creeps in. And like him, I start to sink when I focus more on the storm than on the One who calms it.

Still, I'm learning. When I stop striving and yield to the Spirit's steady breath, I'm carried, not in brief moments, but for longer stretches than I thought possible. There's a stillness up there, a peace that contrasts sharply with the turbulence below. From a spiritual altitude, the world's noise loses some of its power. I see the chaos, yes, but I'm no longer caught in its vortex.

This kind of flight changes how I live on the ground. It's shaping how I approach the health of body, mind, heart, and soul. When I soar, I'm more centered. I breathe deeper. I worry less. I find myself choosing wisdom over reaction, stillness over frenzy. Not because I've mastered anything, but because I've learned to ride something greater than myself.

I don't soar perfectly. Some days, I barely get off the ground. But I return to that verse in Isaiah, not as a distant ideal, but as a lived invitation. And with each attempt, I find the wind is still there, waiting to lift me once again.

Double-Mindedness as a Fence Sitter

I take the Bible's warning about double-mindedness seriously, especially in James 1:5-8: "If any of you lacks wisdom, you should ask God... But when you ask, you must believe and not doubt... That person should not expect to receive anything from the Lord. Such a person is double-minded and unstable in all they do." These words remind me that every thought, word, and decision is a fork in

the road—an invitation to trust Jesus. Whenever I hesitate, trying to keep one foot in faith and the other in self-reliance, I find myself wobbling and easily lured off course by the world's paltry rewards.

Double-mindedness is like perching on a fence, unwilling to commit. On one side lies God's will: on the other, my own. I can study the options, weigh the risks, even pray for guidance. But if I secretly cling to my desire for control, comfort, or success, I'm not truly surrendered. James compares this inner conflict to a wave blown and tossed by the wind. I've lived that image—restless, pulled in two directions, longing for peace but fueling my own instability.

The story of Elijah on Mount Carmel drives this tug-of-war home. He confronted Israel: "How long will you waver between two opinions? If the

Lord is God, follow him; but if Baal is God, follow him" (1 Kings 18:21). That challenge echoes in my own heart. My "Baals" may not be carved idols, but they are just as real: recognition, career, and recognition. Every time I try to serve both God and these masters, I discover the futility of divided worship. Jesus was clear: "No one can serve two masters" (Matthew 6:24).

God's gift of free will allows me to choose: His path or mine. But when I ask Him for wisdom while secretly reserving the right to overrule, I'm not really asking—I'm bargaining. I say I want His peace, yet I withhold surrender. James warns that such a person "should not expect to receive anything from the Lord" (James 1:7). I've seen how quickly anxiety rises when I hedge my trust, and how peace returns only when I lay down my agenda.

The way forward is single-minded devotion. Jesus modeled it in Gethsemane: "Not my will, but yours be done" (Luke 22:42). That is my step down from the fence—choosing His side wholeheartedly. When I trust the All-Knowing God with my decisions, stability returns. My steps are steady. My soul rests. As James 4:8 urges, "Draw near to God, and he will draw near to you... purify your hearts, you double-minded."

I hear that call as deeply personal. God does not want me to wobble between two worlds. He wants my whole heart, my complete allegiance, and my steady footsteps on His path. Each day, I face many fences. Each day, by His grace, I can climb down on His side and walk with Him—no longer divided, but devoted, single-mindedly.

USA as an Apostate Nation

Today is 9/11 Day in the United States—a day that still stirs something deep

in me. It marked a turning point, not just in national security, but in our collective psyche. Evil didn't just strike buildings; it exposed vulnerabilities in our unity, our values, and our spiritual footing. Back then, we rallied around shared grief and a sense of purpose. Today, I'm not sure we'll respond the same way.

The country I once fought for—believing in its role as a beacon of liberty and moral clarity—feels increasingly fragmented. Lady Liberty is certainly in disrepair. We're divided not just by politics, but by economics, race, gender, and a growing list of ideologies that seem to multiply faster than we can make sense of them.

What used to be a shared moral compass rooted in Judeo-Christian principles has been replaced by a kind of moral relativism. Humanism is now the dominant framework, and Dataism—the belief that algorithms and metrics can guide our decisions—is quickly gaining ground, especially among younger generations.

I don't say this to condemn, but because I've felt the shift. Relationships that once felt grounded now feel transactional. Conversations that used to be open and curious are now guarded or performative. Even sincere mention of Jesus can trigger discomfort or dismissal. It's not that people are hostile—it's that they're suspicious of anything that sounds absolute or sacred.

And yet, I've seen signs of hope. Not in sweeping revivals or dramatic conversions, but in quiet moments—older men sharing dreams of a better way, younger people asking more profound questions, communities choosing service over spectacle. Joel 2:28 and Acts 2:17 speak of a time when visions and dreams will guide us again. I don't interpret that as mystical. I see it as a call to reimagine what faith looks like in a fractured world. Perhaps it's less about preaching and more about being present: less about winning arguments and more about living with integrity.

I've started focusing on tangible ways to respond. Listening more. Serving where I can. Writing honestly, even when it costs me. I've accepted that I won't always be understood, and that speaking openly about faith might lead to being sidelined or "canceled." But I don't see that as persecution—I see it as part of the cost of clarity.

America may be drifting, but I haven't given up on her. I believe renewal is possible, not through slogans or policies, but through people choosing depth over distraction. If there's a remnant, it's not defined by numbers— it's determined by conviction. And if I can help reset this nation's moral compass, it is a mission worth fighting for.

Invisible as Made Visible, Part 1

I've been trying to make sense of what it means to know a God I can't see. John 1:18 says, "No one has ever seen God; the only God, who is at the Father's side, he has made him known."

I interpret this passage as God's essence is so incomprehensible that only Jesus, the manifestation of the Almighty, was begotten to show us what He's like. Before I knew Jesus, the notion of an intermediary seemed unnecessary for a God of love. Other religions advocate going directly to the source rather than through a subordinate, but Christianity does not.

When I reread Exodus 33:20 —"You cannot see my face, for man shall not see me and live"—I no longer interpret it as a threat. I see it as a protective

boundary. God's holiness is too vast, too otherworldly for direct sight. It reminds me of moments when life's questions feel too big to hold. In these times, I stopped trying to grasp everything and leaned into prayer for understanding, discernment, and, above all, patience. I talk to Jesus like an older brother or mentor who understands my questions and can explain God's greatness.

The Holy Spirit helps me. When I'm journaling or walking, I get quiet nudges—gentle reminders to trust what I can't see. 1 Timothy 6:16 says God dwells in "unapproachable light, whom no one has ever seen or can see." A light that is so blinding that I equate it to a nuclear blast.

When I was practicing nuclear weapon delivery tactics in my F-4 Phantom fighter aircraft, on egress, I was taught to place my helmet bag over my head to keep the flash from the explosion from destroying the retinas in my eyes. It's why I rely on the Spirit to guide my thoughts about the Almighty and keep me safe from overexposure, even if I naively consider myself bulletproof.

Invisibility isn't a barrier. It's part of how I build faith. John 4:24 states that God is spirit, so worship occurs in spirit and truth, not through visuals. For me, that means starting my day with thanks, not needing proof, but feeling connected to Jesus through the power of the Spirit. They make the Father known without overwhelming me, nourishing me with spiritual tidbits.

Psalm 27:8 says, "You have said, 'Seek my face.' My heart says to you, 'Your face, Lord, do I seek.'" That longing isn't about physical sight. It's about spiritual insight. I interpret it as a call to lean in, even when clarity is elusive.

These verses encourage me to keep seeking without expecting full sight but insight. In contemplation, I sit with the mystery, letting the Holy Spirit illuminate it gradually. It's not about solving a mystery but walking with it, day by day. Jesus bridges the gap, turning what I can't see into something I can experience.

Invisible as Made Visible, Part 2

Building on those thoughts about God's invisibility, I've been reflecting on

Jesus as the liaison who reveals the Father. John 6:46 says, "Not that anyone has seen the Father except he who is from God; he has seen the Father." This passage says "seen" as opposed to "know." While I can't see the Father, I am capable of knowing Him by, in, and through His begotten (not created) Son.

Being begotten by the Father means that He is entirely like His Father—not like an identical twin, but of the same essence—in a physical way I can comprehend. When I internalize this passage, it's as if Jesus is saying, "I've got the inside view," and that helps me better comprehend and "visualize" the invisible Father in an abstract way. In today's techno-speak, the Father morphed Himself into a form that this lowly being could understand—without being alarmed by His unspeakable presence or harmed by His incredible power.

Hebrews 1:3 refers to Jesus as the "exact representation" of God's being. Thus, if I genuinely want to know the Father, I must incorporate Jesus' words and actions. In quiet moments, I reread stories like the Sermon on the

Mount. His teachings on forgiveness and mercy don't feel lofty—they feel like advice from someone who has walked His talk.

John 14:8-9 is another anchor. Philip asks to see the Father, and Jesus replies, "Whoever has seen me has seen the Father." That reassures me. In stressful moments—whether it's work pressure or family tension—I remember that Jesus makes the invisible Father approachable. I don't need to strain to see God; I need to stay close to Jesus.

Colossians 1:15 calls Jesus "the image of the invisible God, the firstborn of all creation." As firstborn, He preceded not only Adam but the angels. He sets the standard for all beings, material and immaterial. This passage clearly indicates that Jesus is the perfect representation of His Father and that I don't need to look any further to see an invisible God. In Him, the invisible just became visible.

The Holy Spirit helps me apply this. John 16:13-15 states that the Spirit guides us into truth, drawing from Jesus and making it personal. For me, that's like getting unexpected clarity during Bible study or while doing something mundane. A verse clicks, and I see how it threads back to God's heart. I don't force it—it just comes, often when I'm not trying.

This perspective keeps things balanced. I interpret these verses as invitations to a relationship rather than riddles. Jesus' presence makes faith livable. Without Him, the Father's invisibility might feel distant. But through daily interactions—such as reading, praying, listening—I experience God in ways that are real and deeply personal to me.

Invisible as Made Visible, Part 3

Wrapping up these Invisible as Made Visible reflections, I've been thinking about how this all plays out in my life now—and in the future.

Apostle Paul used the phrase "seeing through a glass darkly" (1 Corinthians 13:12) as a metaphor to contrast our current understanding of God's nature and the essence of reality with the future clarity and insight that will be achieved upon union with God. That phrase resonates with me. It's not just hopeful—it's inspiring. I live in the fog now, but I trust the light ahead.

2 Corinthians 4:6 says God has "shone in our hearts to give the light of the knowledge of the glory of God in the face of Jesus Christ." God is light, and Jesus is the light of this world. As a disciple, Jesus expects me to reflect Their light. 2 Corinthians 4:7 says we have "treasure in jars of clay." While I'm ordinary, I carry something valuable. When I help a neighbor or show patience, it's God abiding in action.

As 1 John 4:12 states, "No one has ever seen God; if we love one another, God lives in us, and his love is made complete in us." God is love, and tapping into His unending source of love makes the invisible visible.

Isaiah 9:6 calls the future Jesus, "Wonderful Counselor," and that's how I experience Him—someone who doesn't just speak truth but walks me through it. I thank Him for showing the Father without the danger of direct sight. It builds trust. Now, I don't need to see to believe.

Revelation 22:4 looks ahead to seeing God's face, but for now, it's through faith. I am content knowing God, even though I have not seen Him fully. Faith shapes my days, as I choose hope over worry and grace over frustration.

John 14:26 says the Spirit teaches and reminds us of Jesus' words. For me, that's practical—quiet nudges during chores, linking back to Scripture. A verse I read days ago suddenly seems to fit a situation I'm facing. It's not mystical—it's real.

With Jesus, it's an ongoing dialogue. I interpret moments like the Transfiguration in Matthew 17:1-8 as glimpses rather than the norm. In my life, that means appreciating small revelations—like sensing forgiveness after falling short. Looking ahead, I trust the promise of full sight without fear. Until then, I rely on Jesus' revelation and the Spirit's presence. It's a quiet journey, built on trust. I don't need to see everything—I need to stay faithful with what I've been shown.

This series of reflections strengthens my faith. Interpreting these verses personally, I see God's plan as relational. Through daily prayer and obedience, the invisible Father feels close—not through visions or dramatic signs, but through small, steady moments of connection. It's a walk, not a sprint. And in that walk, the unseen becomes visible—not to my eyes, but to my heart.

Jesus as a Pioneer

As a child watching westerns on TV, I was fascinated by trailblazers like Daniel Boone and Davy Crockett. Their courage and grit stirred something within me, a longing to venture into the unknown. In pilot training, I was given the honor of selecting an airplane of my choice. To my new wife's dismay, I chose an F-105G Wild Weasel fighter used for the hazardous SEAD mission in  Vietnam. Trailblazing Wild Weasel pilots suppressed enemy air defense systems (SEAD), including surface-to-air missiles and anti-aircraft artillery, thereby clearing the way for other aircraft to operate more freely and effectively—much like Jesus clears the path for me today.

The Bible doesn't directly refer to Jesus as a "pioneer" in the modern sense, but several passages describe Him as one who goes ahead, leads the way, or prepares a path for others. This imagery resonates with me deeply. Hebrews 2:10 calls Jesus "the founder and perfecter of our faith," a leader, originator, or one who goes first. Hebrews 12:2 echoes this theme: "the founder and perfecter of our faith, who for the joy that was set before him endured the cross, despising the shame, and is seated at the right hand of the throne of God." This verse paints Jesus as the ultimate trailblazer—one who endured suffering to complete the journey of faith for all who follow. Though He suffered, His path remained steady and sure.

Pioneering resonates deeply with me, drawing parallels to those Wild Weasel missions where pilots ventured into peril to pave the way for others. Just as I aspired to lead in the skies, Jesus embodies the ultimate pioneer, facing suffering to guide humanity toward glory. His leadership is not merely strategic—it is sacrificial. Contemplating this, I see how His role extends beyond mere leadership—He initiates a divine path, perfected through His own trials.

Hebrews 6:20 adds the term "forerunner," referring to one who enters God's holy presence first, thereby securing our hope like an anchor in stormy seas. In my military days, scouting ahead meant risking everything to ensure the squadron's safety. In a far greater sense, Jesus breaches the veil of separation between God and man, inviting us to follow Him without fear.

John 10:2 depicts the Good Shepherd leading from the front, His voice a beacon in times of uncertainty. In John 14:2, Jesus assures me that He will go and prepare a place for me—just as a pioneer forges ahead to ready a refuge. His promise to return and guide me home reminds me of comrades who cleared hostile territories so others could advance.

These scriptures weave a tapestry of Jesus as a pioneer—going ahead, enduring, preparing. In quiet moments, I ponder how my aspirations could mirror His trailblazing. Jesus is not only the pioneer of my faith—He is the trailblazer of my heart.

Jesus as a Friend

When I think of Jesus as Savior, King, Shepherd, even as Lord, there's a natural reverence that rises in me. But friend? That one catches in my throat. It feels too familiar, too intimate for someone so immeasurably greater than I am.

I know He said it—"You are my friends if you do what I command" (John 15:14). Not just once, but clearly and directly. He even explained that He moved me from servant to friend because He shared with me the heart of the Father (John 15:15). That's not me assuming too much—that's Him extending the invitation. And still, part of me feels unworthy like an ant being invited into the confidence of an elephant. The scale doesn't make sense. I suppose that's the point.

Jesus isn't asking me to meet Him in His grandeur. He's stepping into my smallness with gentleness and knowing. He's the kind of friend who doesn't need anything from me yet chooses to offer everything to me—including Himself. I didn't initiate this—He did. "You did not choose me, but I chose you," He says in John 15:16. That alone is enough to drop me to my knees or shed a tear despite my bravado.

But Jesus didn't just choose me for friendship. He appointed me to bear fruit—real, lasting, spiritual fruit. He even gave me access to the Father for the resources to do it. Ask in My name, He says. Not for selfish gain, but to carry out the love He modeled.

And that's the condition, if you can call it one: Love one another as I have loved you (John 15:12). Not halfway love. Not polite love. Self-giving, grace-willing love. That's what keeps this friendship alive.

I've learned that this isn't a friendship of equals, and it never was meant to be. It's more like being brought into confidence by a sovereign who is tender beyond all reason. He calls me friend, not to flatten the roles, but to pull me into His purpose.

I try to obey—not out of fear, but out of gratitude. I want to be the kind of friend who listens, who follows, who delights in whatever draws me closer to Him. And still, there are days I fall short. He knows that. And yet He keeps calling me back. Not a servant. Not a stranger. Friend.

So maybe friendship with Jesus isn't a matter of worthiness at all—it's a matter of willing hearts. Hearts that say, "I don't understand why You'd choose me, but I won't walk away from the gift."

And maybe, just maybe, He smiles at that. Because friendship, real friendship always begins with trust.

Weakness as Made Perfect

I used to think strength was something I had to muster—something earned through discipline, resilience, or sheer will. But the longer I walk this path, the more I find myself undone by the quiet truth: weakness, when surrendered, becomes the very place God chooses to dwell.

Paul's words in 2 Corinthians 12:9-10 echo louder in me now than they once did: "My grace is sufficient for you, for my power is made perfect in weakness." I used to read that as a form of consolation. Now I receive it as an invitation. The thorn in Paul's flesh— whatever it was—wasn't removed. And mine, too, remains. But I've stopped asking for it to be taken. Not because I've grown numb, but because I've begun to see how it draws me nearer to the One who does not despise frailty.

Isaiah 40:29–31 speaks of renewed strength, not manufactured strength. "He gives power to the faint." That line alone feels like a crutch. I don't need to pretend I'm strong when I feel weak. I need lifting. And in Him, I find myself lifted—not always out of the circumstance, but into a posture of trust. Wings like eagles aren't always visible. Sometimes they're simply the grace to accept a helping hand to stand when I fail or fall.

Hebrews 11:34 reminds me that some were "made strong out of weakness." Not beside it. Not despite it. That phrase—"out of weakness"—reshapes my understanding. Weakness isn't the obstacle to strength—it's the soil from which it grows. I think of Gideon, of David, of Rahab. None of them fit the mold of worldly power. And yet, they were chosen. Used. Honored.

2 Corinthians 4:7 calls me a jar of clay. I used to resist that image. Clay cracks. It's fragile. But now I see the beauty in it. The treasure isn't the vessel itself, but what it holds. "This all-surpassing power is from God and not from us." That truth frees me. I don't have to shine. I have to be open.

Romans 5:6 says Christ died for the ungodly while we were still weak. That verse doesn't flatter—it humbles. He didn't wait for me to clean up. He came when I was most unworthy. That kind of love doesn't just redeem— it redefines.

Hebrews 4:15 is the passage I return to when I feel most exposed: "We do not have a high priest who is unable to sympathize with our weaknesses." Jesus knows. Not abstractly. Personally. So I approach the throne—not with polished prayers, but with trembling honesty. And I find mercy.

I write this not as someone who has arrived, but as someone still learning to lean on God, my refuge and ultimate source of strength.

Life as a Mason Jar

During the COVID-19 lockdown, I spent months confined to my home, a world reduced to four walls and a flickering screen. It felt like I was living in a Mason jar—sealed off, peering at life through smudged glass.

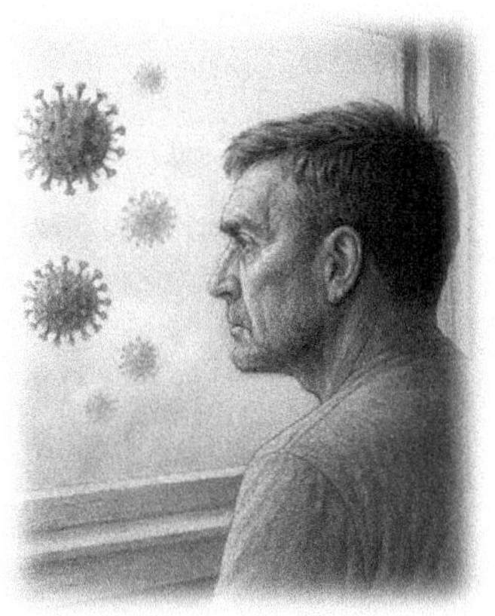

Zoom calls and news feeds offered glimpses of the outside, but the enjoyment of others and the bustle of crowds remained beyond reach. This isolation, both physical and sensory, mirrored my earthly existence: limited, fragile, yet brimming with divine purpose.

Scripture likens me to "jars of clay," fragile vessels holding divine treasure, showing God's power through my weakness (2 Cor 4:7). I am preserved in a closed earthly ecosystem, bound by time and space, my understanding filtered through my five senses—sight, hearing, touch, taste, smell. These gifts, miraculous yet finite, also confine me. A virtual concert streams colors, pungent odors, and melodies, but still within a bubble that encompasses my Mason jar, my family members' jars, and a few associates. Misinformation clouds my view, like fingerprints on the jar's glass. As Paul writes, we "see through a glass darkly," my vision partial until divine clarity dawns (1 Cor 13:12).

Technology and connections with fellow "Mason Jarers" stretch my reach— social media shares joys, telecasts bridge distances—but these are shadows of reality, easily distorted. A manipulated headline can skew truth, like a warped lens. Yet the spiritual realm transcends such bounds, much like the digital world, where data flows instantly across borders. God, eternal, exists beyond time: "From everlasting to everlasting, you are God" (Ps 90:2). His perspective dwarfs mine—"a day is like a thousand years" (2 Pet 3:8)—offering wisdom unbound by my sensory jar.

This confinement calls me to submit to God's will, as clay shaped by the potter (Jer 18:6). Seeking His infinite plan guides me through the fog, illuminating paths for loved ones who share my dim sight. Modern terms like "carbon-based units" or "meat sacks" echo ancient truths of frailty, akin to grass that withers (Isa 40:6-8). Our jars, though cracked, hold divine light, reflecting purpose amid limitation.

The jar's lid—sealed by mortality—awaits God's hand to unscrew it: "When the perishable has been clothed with the imperishable, death is swallowed up in victory" (1 Cor 15:54). Until that moment, we embrace the jar's purpose: to preserve faith, I see light shine through fractures and anticipate liberation of His eternal promise.

My quarantine days taught me this—confinement, though stifling, fosters reliance on the Divine, transforming isolation into a sacred time to concentrate on God. In this divine analogy, each Mason jar, however fragile, is a vessel of hope, awaiting the day God opens the lid to reveal His infinite design.

Life as Viewed from a Cockpit

From the vantage point of a fighter jet cockpit, where I've logged over 4,000 hours soaring at supersonic speeds, life below unfolded like a divine panorama.

Strapped into that confined space—no larger than a closet—I commanded an unparalleled "God's-eye view" of sprawling cities, rivers snaking through valleys, and storms brewing. Instruments augmented my senses with heads-up displays overlaying data on the windshield. Yet this elevated perspective was fleeting, a series of fragmented snapshots distorted by speed, altitude, and the canopy's glare. It was a privileged glimpse, superior to earthbound eyes, but ultimately limited, echoing our human sojourn: a brief flight through existence, perceiving reality in partial frames.

Scripture portrays us as fragile vessels, "jars of clay" cradling divine treasure, revealing God's power through our frailty (2 Cor 4:7). In the cockpit of life, we're pilots navigating with restricted instruments. Our five senses filter the world, and technology extends our reach but not our depth. A satellite feed might relay global events, yet it lacks the intimate pulse of lives touched, skewed by incomplete intel or atmospheric interference. As Paul reflects, we "see through a glass darkly": our vision hazy and incomplete until we behold face to face (1 Cor 13:12). My aerial view captures broad strokes but misses the subtle workings of providence below.

Contrast my limited view with the boundless vista through Jesus' all-seeing eyes and the Holy Spirit's illuminating lens. God transcends our cockpit confines, eternal and omnipresent: "From everlasting to everlasting, you are God" (Ps 90:2). His gaze spans epochs—"a day is like a thousand years" (2 Pet 3:8)—penetrating souls with unerring clarity, unbound by time or space. The Spirit, like an infinite heads-up display, reveals truths our mortal instruments cannot detect, guiding with wisdom that defies fragmentation.

This realization humbles me, urging me to submit to the ultimate Pilot. Like clay molded by the potter (Jer 18:6), we yield control, trusting His flight plan amid turbulence. Through prayer and Scripture, we align our fragmented views with His panoramic vision, leading loved ones who navigate their own hazy cockpits. Modern metaphors—humans as "carbon-based units" or fleeting "data streams"—echo ancient frailty, akin to grass that withers (Isa 40:6-8). Yet, in our cockpits, divine light filters through cracks, offering purpose in the partial.

The mission's end promises to debrief in eternity's hangar: "When the perishable has been clothed with the imperishable, death is swallowed up in victory" (1 Cor 15:54). Until then, I cherish the cockpit's lessons—embrace the fragments, let the Spirit refine the view, and anticipate the day we see fully, unfiltered, through Christ's eyes.

Works as a Yardstick

Faith alone opens the door to salvation, but good works serve as the yardstick that gauges my commitment to Christ, my Cornerstone, revealing how deeply I love God and others. Love defines God Himself—"God is love" (1 John 4:8)—and should characterize my life as a believer. As a warrior at heart, I find it challenging to learn to love selflessly with agape love in this hate-filled world, where my instinctive response is to confront rather than forgive.

When I reflect on my past self, I was judgmental, quick to anger, and prone to verbal and physical confrontations, depending on the situation. Faith was God's gift that pulled me from that pit. But good works testify that my faith is alive. James 2:18 puts it bluntly: "Show me your faith apart from your works, and I will show you my faith by my works." It's a reminder that my actions must align with my beliefs. James also bluntly concludes his letter with a warning: "Faith without works is dead." (James 2:26). Ephesians 2:8-10 also reminds me that I'm saved by grace, not by works, but continues by saying God "created me to do good works in Christ Jesus". My efforts don't earn salvation, but they reveal what's being cultivated in my heart.

Matthew 5:16 hits home: "Let your light shine before others, so that they may see your good deeds and glorify your Father in heaven." In my quieter moments, I notice how small choices—like helping someone without expecting thanks or staying calm when I'd rather snap—mark my progress.

They're not grand gestures; they're daily steps that show love and help me overcome my old instincts. Choosing kindness over payback marks another inch forward, proving my commitment is real. James 2:14 challenges me: "What good is it if someone claims to have faith but has no deeds?" It compels me to evaluate whether my actions reflect my faith continually.

When threatened, most people's visceral reaction is to flee. Verbal or physical threats trigger my fight response. As a former tip-of-spear combatant, this instinct could be deadly. In the past, when offended, retribution was the first thought that entered my mind. Today, that same thought activates my fight mode. However, the Spirit within me quickly intercedes. As a young Christian, I often overruled the Spirit and suffered the consequences. As a more mature follower, Jesus has trained me to restrain—not eliminate—that inner beast and pursue more rational outcomes. His agape love calls for forgiveness, even toward the one who hurt me. It's tough, but those moments shape me. Good works are measured now in yards instead of inches. Someday, I pray that mile markers will replace my yardstick.

I stumble—old habits die hard—but Jesus knows I can't walk without tripping. He arranged with the Father to send the Holy Spirit to remind me of everything He taught (John 14:26) and empower me to walk with confidence. I'm not perfect, but each piece of good work marks my transformation from that angry man into someone who pursues God's will and reflects Jesus' love.

Jesus as Living Water

Recently, I have been reflecting on Jesus as living water and on how the Holy Spirit purifies what He provides so that I can lead an abundant and healthy life. That reflection has drawn me back to my years in high-tech water management—developing systems that transform polluted water into a clean, drinkable source of life. These ventures weren't just commercial; they were personal. I've always seen clean water as a sacred provision, a gift meant to sustain life. And when I consider the spiritual parallels, I find myself drawn to the Holy Spirit's role in purifying the soul—much like those systems purify the water we consume.

In John 4, Jesus meets a Samaritan woman at Jacob's well. She comes for

physical water, but He offers something far deeper: "Whoever drinks the water I give them will never thirst. Indeed, the water I give them will become in them a spring of water welling up to eternal life" (John 4:14). That moment wasn't about revelation but restoration. Jesus didn't shame her history; He invited her into renewal. The agent of that renewal, the living water, is the Holy Spirit.

Just as polluted water must pass through membranes, filters, and UV light to be made clean, our hearts—clouded by pride, pain, and distortion—require the Spirit's refining presence, not in a mystical or overly spiritualized way, but in the quiet, daily work of conviction, comfort, and clarity. The Spirit doesn't just cleanse; He restores us to the purity God intended for me.

In Ezekiel 36:25–27, God promises, "I will sprinkle clean water on you, and you will be clean... I will give you a new heart and put a new spirit in you." That passage echoes the same theme: purification precedes transformation. And in Isaiah 12:3, we're told, "With joy you will draw water from the wells of salvation." Again, the metaphor is not abstract. Water is essential, and so is the Spirit's work in making us whole.

I've seen firsthand how contaminated water can be made safe to drink again. It takes intentional design, rigorous testing, and constant flow. Likewise, the Spirit's purification isn't a one-time event. It's an ongoing and iterative process. He doesn't just remove the obvious toxins; He reaches into the hidden places, the sediment of our soul, and filters them through grace.

The woman at the well left her jar behind. That detail matters. She came for water, but she found something better. And in doing so, she became a vessel herself—carrying the news of living water to her village. That's the invitation for me, too. Not to be perfect, but to be purified. Not to be the source, but to be a vessel through which the Spirit flows. And in that vesselhood, I've found that the Holy Spirit continually refreshes me with the living water that Jesus provides—cleansing, sustaining, and renewing me day by day.

Stupid as an Ignoramus

As I have matured in my faith, I have learned that to ignore is ignorant, and a clueless, stupid person is an ignoramus, especially when they disregard God. The word "ignore" comes from the Latin *ignorare*, meaning "to not know" or "to be unacquainted with." To be ignorant, therefore, is not merely to lack knowledge, but to actively choose not to know—to disregard, shun, or spurn something of someone. This is a spiritual truth with consequences in our daily lives, and on a cosmic scale.

Ignoring others is not only rude but also hurtful. When we choose to ignore someone, we deny their existence and worth. It's a form of spiritual blindness that prevents us from seeing the divine in every individual. Jesus is clear about the importance of acknowledging and caring for one another: "Truly I tell you, whatever you did for one of the least of these brothers and sisters of mine, you did for me" (Matt 25:40). To ignore a person in need is to ignore Christ himself.

To ignore our own mental, emotional, physical, and spiritual health is unhealthy and equally ignorant. We are created as whole beings, and neglecting any part of ourselves leads to a breakdown of the entire system. Paul urges us to treat our bodies as temples of the Holy Spirit (1 Cor 6:19). Neglecting our spiritual health, in particular, is a profound act of ignorance. It's like owning a priceless treasure and letting it decay. When we ignore the spiritual discipline of prayer, reading Scripture, and communion with God, we are deliberately choosing to live in spiritual poverty. The Bible often connects wisdom with health and foolishness with decay, reminding us that true wellness comes from living in alignment with God's will.

To ignore God is not only sinful, but it will lead to damnation at the Day of Judgment. This is the most profound and dangerous form of ignorance. The Bible leaves no room for ambiguity in this matter. The psalmist declares, "The fool says in his heart, 'There is no God'" (Ps 14:1). Ignoring God's existence and His call to repentance is the ultimate act of self-deception. It is a willful blindness that culminates in eternal separation from the source of life. The prophet Hosea famously laments, "My people are destroyed from lack of knowledge" (Hos 4:6), not because they couldn't know God, but because they actively chose to reject His knowledge.

The Bible makes it clear that there is no excuse for such ignorance. The Apostle Paul, in his letter to the Romans, explains that God's eternal power and divine nature have been clearly seen through what has been made, "so that people are without excuse" (Rom 1:20). The creation itself is a testimony to the Creator, and to ignore it is an act of deliberate spiritual ignorance. Only an ignoramus would shun these Biblical truths.

Jesus as the Only Way

While most Christians affirm the New Testament teaching that salvation comes through Jesus Christ alone (e.g., John 14:6: "I am the way, the truth, and the life. No one comes to the Father except through me," and Acts 4:12: "There is salvation in no one else")—a truth I uphold—I also believe these verses should be viewed within the broader context that the Bible provides.

My Jewish and Muslim colleagues often ask me about the exclusivity of  these verses. During a conversation with a Muslim cleric, he referenced Romans 8:14: "For all who the Spirit of God leads are sons of God," implying that non-Christians who are spiritually oriented may also attain heaven. Similarly, my Rabbi friends remind me that Jews are God's chosen people, Jesus was Jewish, and my Bible depicts Christians as wild olive shoots (Romans 11) that can be grafted onto a Jewish olive tree amongst Jewish branches. These clerics also challenge a theology that excludes people who have never heard of Jesus.

To fellow Christians, I assert that Jesus imposes the highest standard for those who have received the "Word." More than others, Christians must be steadfast in their faith as they follow His challenging path of testing and transformation. Jesus told His disciples that many believers—five of ten bridesmaids, two of three servants with talents, and four of five in the sowing parable—will fail to make it through the "narrow gate," and those who find it are few. Thus, enduring faith in Christ is the explicit path to sonship. It's framed as a right granted to those who respond to His leadership regardless of ethnicity or religious label (Revelation 21:7).

Regarding Jews, Hosea said, "...in the place where it was said to them, 'You are not my people,' it shall be said to them, 'Children of the living God,'" which is tantamount to saying that those once excluded will be called sons. In Protestant circles, Jews, like all people, must place explicit faith in Jesus as the Messiah for salvation and entry into heaven. From my standpoint, religious Jews are awaiting their Messiah, who comes from the line of David—namely, Jesus. Catholic theology affirms that salvation is through Christ alone but holds that God's covenant with the Jews is irrevocable. "All Israel will be saved...the calling of God is irrevocable" (Romans 11:26).

Regarding Muslims, I have spent hundreds of hours pointing out scriptures in the Quran to Muslim clerics about Jesus, who is mentioned 25 times, more than the Prophet Muhammad. His name is Isa bin Maryam (Jesus, son of Mary, the only woman mentioned in the Quran by name) and is called "Messiah" 11 times. The Quran affirms His divine birth, Him as the "Word" of God and the only "sinless" man, and foretells His divine return. Muslims are also taught to believe in the Gospels (Injeel), which God revealed to Jesus as guidance and light (Sura 5:46).

Given this information, I still hold the view that all must go through Jesus on the Day of Judgment. My All-Knowing Savior will likely save those who do not know Him but earnestly seek God, striving to do His Father's will, purpose, and glory. Moreover, He will show the same compassion to children, invalids, mentally-challenged, and even those possessed by demons as He did when He walked on earth.

Great Shepherd as the Sacrificial Lamb

To me, the image of a shepherd, strong and watchful, guarding his flock, has always evoked a vivid picture of Christ. It speaks of divine care, guidance, and protection. Yet within the profound tapestry of Christian theology, this majestic figure, the Great Shepherd, assumes an astonishing and deeply moving role: that of a Sacrificial Lamb. How can the one who leads, protects, and ultimately governs also be the one who is led, exposed, and sacrificed? This is the core of the paradox—the Almighty God, manifest in Christ, who shepherds humanity, willingly becoming the vulnerable, spotless Lamb.

The Old Testament's repeated call for perfect, unblemished lambs for sacrifice underscores the purity required for true atonement. And here, in Jesus, we find not just physical perfection, but a sinless life, a righteousness that far surpasses any human endeavor—a purity essential for the ultimate sacrifice. I must admit that I am a testament to the need for such a sacrifice.

My shortcomings are numerous. I frequently stumble, not just in action, but in thought and intention. The weight of these imperfections, these acts of turning away from the Shepherd's path, would be crushing were it not for the divine solution presented in the Lamb. This is where the concepts of expiation and propitiation become not just theological terms, but my lifelines.

Expiation removes my sin. Imagine a debt so vast it could never be repaid, or a stain so deep it seems impossible to remove. Expiation is the act of paying that debt. Christ's death on the cross serves as the ultimate payment for the penalty of my sins. He bore the full consequence, the just punishment, effectively erasing the record of my transgressions. For me, this means that the guilt and burden of my prideful actions and failures are not merely overlooked but removed.

Then there is propitiation. Because God is perfectly holy, He cannot simply ignore sin; His just nature requires a response to evil. Propitiation, then, is the act by which Christ's death endured the righteous wrath of God on my behalf. His suffering on the cross satisfied divine justice and appeased God's anger toward my sin. It's like a storm of divine justice, rightfully aimed at my rebellion, was entirely absorbed by the Great Shepherd who became the Lamb.

The Great Shepherd, by becoming the Sacrificial Lamb, transformed my bleak prospect of divine judgment into an offering of grace. He who guides me through life has also taken my place on the altar, allowing me to be reconciled to a holy God. This profound act ensures that my shortcomings—which would otherwise separate me eternally—are met with boundless mercy. This paradox is the most beautiful expression of God's love for His flawed creation, offering removal of sin and restoration of relationship through the loving sacrifice of the Lamb.

Jesus as the Ultimate Blessing, Part 1

Looking back on my life, there is no doubt that Jesus is the greatest blessing I have ever received. Like most people, I was familiar with the famous verse in John 3:16: "For God so loved the world that he gave his one and only Son, that whoever believes in him shall not perish but have eternal life." Still, I didn't truly internalize it until I surrendered my life to Christ. By yielding my will to His, He began to create new life and purpose within me. A grain of wheat must fall to the ground and die to bear much fruit (John 12:24). I am living evidence of that fruit.

As I matured in Christ, these scriptures came alive. "Blessed be the God and

Father of our Lord Jesus Christ, who has blessed us in Christ with every spiritual blessing in the heavenly places" (Ephesians 1:3) reveals how Jesus channels all divine favor to us. Another is 1 John 3:16-18: "This is how we know what love is: Jesus Christ laid down his life for us. And we ought to lay down our lives for our brothers and sisters." John 11:25-26 adds: "I am the resurrection and the life. Whoever believes in me, though he die, yet shall he live, and everyone who lives and believes in me shall never die." These verses reinforce Jesus as the centerpiece of God's ultimate blessing toward people like me—once an angry young man on a path to destruction.

Picture a dysfunctional family after the death of a cherished father at age 36—that was mine. As the oldest of three children, I was deeply entangled in the mess: angry, withdrawn, and moody. I carried these burdens until I was 30, by then married to my high school sweetheart, who saw something worthwhile in me—even as I carried the emotional weight of thousands of souls I had taken in combat. By worldly standards, I was a successful, up-and-coming young man—highly decorated, with a beautiful wife and a promising career. But by heavenly standards, I was hollow, chasing fulfillment in all the wrong places.

Then imagine a family member stepping in not with a quick fix or a lecture, but by entering the chaos and sacrificing their own comfort to rebuild what was broken. That's Jesus to me. He didn't just point the way. He became the way, stepping into my life with a compassion so deep that it seeped through my hardened shell like osmosis of living water. Eventually, I realized that God was giving His Son to rewrite my story—and to give me a new conscience, shaped by His Spirit.

This blessing reshaped me. Where anger once ruled, I found peace. Jesus' gift brought redirection, purpose, and a hope that outlasts this life. It's like that family member who teaches new skills, repairs the home, and models a better way to live. I'm not perfect, but I'm different—less selfish, more patient, and striving to reflect that same love to others. In tough times, when doubts creep in, or life feels heavy, I lean on Jesus. He is not only my Lord—He is my constant companion.

Jesus as the Ultimate Blessing, Part 2

Jesus is the ultimate channel for divine favor, as Ephesians 3 reveals in Paul's words: "For this reason I, Paul, the prisoner of Christ Jesus for the sake of you Gentiles—" He explains the mystery that through the gospel, outsiders like the Gentiles become co-heirs, part of one body, sharing in God's promises through Christ. Reflecting on my own life, I was once that outsider, but Jesus bridged the gap, delivering His Father's kindness to me, not because I earned it, but because He chose to lead me out of darkness.

Divine favor is God's unearned kindness, a grace that shows His love in real, everyday ways. It's not about deserving it; it's like a gift that opens doors or brings calm when life feels heavy. Scripture gives clear examples. There's forgiveness, like Ephesians 1:7 says, "In him we have redemption through his blood, the forgiveness of sins, in accordance with the riches of God's grace," wiping clean the record of my past. Or peace that holds steady in chaos, as Philippians 4:7 promises, guarding my heart and mind in Christ. Provision also shows up, like unexpected help when I've needed it, echoing Matthew 6:33 about seeking God's kingdom first. And protection, as Psalm 5:12 notes, "Surely, Lord, you bless the righteous; you surround them with your favor as with a shield."

I've seen these in my life—second chances, calm in storms, needs met out of nowhere—blessings I couldn't orchestrate or deserve.

Divine favor, often synonymous with grace, is the unmerited kindness and blessing bestowed by God upon individuals. It is a central theme in the Bible, reflecting God's benevolence and love towards humanity. I envision this as a man struggling on a road to destruction. Then a family member steps in, not just to help, but as the sole heir of a wealthy patriarch, channeling all the estate's resources—land, wisdom, support—directly to me. This person lives with me, clears my debts, and teaches me how to thrive. That's Jesus.

Galatians 2:20puts it plainly: "It is no longer I who live, but Christ lives in me." Furthermore, Jesus continually reminds me that "I am in my Father, and you in Me, and I in you!" (John 14.20). Now God's favor flows through Him into me as long as I seek His will in Jesus. Jesus entered my soul, died to settle my score, and now distributes grace, making me an heir to promises I couldn't have claimed otherwise.

This changed how I live. Knowing favor comes through Christ humbles me—it's not my doing. I've seen it in action: a job when I was desperate, a mended friendship when I thought it was gone. It compels me to share that same kindness, to listen more attentively, and to give without expecting anything in return, because that's how Jesus treats me. In tough times—doubt, loss, or fear—I lean on Him as the steady source of favor, turning scarcity into enough. It's not flashy; it's a quiet strength that keeps me going. I'm just thankful and in awe of a God who channels everything good through His Son, transforming someone like me.

Immaterial as Material (Theophanies)

I am drawn to the mystery of theophanies—temporary manifestations of God tailored to human perception. They do not alter His eternal nature but serve as bridges between the divine and the tangible realm. In Scripture, these moments often carry a distinct purpose: to guide, to commission, or to affirm His presence. For decades, my spiritual vision was veiled. Now, through the eyes of Jesus and the lens of the Holy Spirit, I perceive them with increasing clarity.

The most famous theophany appears in Exodus 3, where God appeared to

Moses from a burning bush that was not consumed. From within the flames, He spoke, identified Himself as "I AM WHO I AM," and called Moses to lead His people. This encounter merges visual wonder with divine authority.

In Exodus 13–14, God guides the Israelites through the wilderness by day as a pillar of cloud and by night as a pillar of fire—a visible sign of His protection and direction. At Mount Sinai, His presence descends in thunder, lightning, and smoke, declaring His holiness as He delivers the Ten Commandments. In 2 Kings 2, Elijah is taken up in a whirlwind accompanied by chariots of fire—

a dramatic departure that affirms God's sovereignty over life and death. These events share a common thread: God revealing Himself in ways that evoke reverence and demand response.

Today, I experience God's presence through the indwelling of the Holy Spirit, as promised in John 14:16-17. This is no longer a fleeting encounter but a continual reality. I sense Him in moments of peace during hardship, as described in Philippians 4:7 as the "peace of God that transcends all understanding", or through conviction that prompts change, aligning with John 16:8's "He (Jesus) will convict the world of sin, and of righteousness and judgment". Scripture often speaks directly to my situation, illuminating truth like a lamp to my feet (Psalm 119:105). In prayer, I receive quiet nudges toward action or insight, echoing Romans 8:26's admonition that the Holy Spirit helps me in my weakness. Through community, a timely word or act of kindness can reveal divine direction, much like the Spirit's work in the Acts of the Apostles.

These manifestations may not come with fire or thunder, but they build faith steadily. They teach me to look for God not only in the extraordinary but also in the ordinary—through inner promptings, scriptural clarity, and relational confirmation.

In contemplating theophanies, I find encouragement. What once felt distant now feels near. May I continue to seek and recognize His presence, trusting that He still reveals Himself to those who are learning to see the immaterial becoming material through theophanies—and on rare occasions, through a Christophany: a manifestation of Christ Himself.

Immaterial as Material (Christophanies)

As a follow-up to theophanies, I've come to appreciate the unique category of Christophanies or appearances of the pre-incarnate Son of God, Jesus Christ. These are not general manifestations of God, but specific revelations of the eternal Son before His birth in Bethlehem.

As I mentioned in previous Divine Analogies, I experienced a Christophany of Jesus Himself in Japan, where He appeared to me as an apparition that led to my conversion. This event was confirmed by a Christian friend, who called me at the exact moment Christ appeared.

Christophanies are a subset of theophanies, but they carry distinct markers, such as authoritative speech, divine knowledge, and human-like interaction, that bridge heaven and earth. These appearances do not compromise Christ's divine nature; instead, they reveal His role as mediator and messenger. By studying them, I've learned more about Jesus, then and now.

One of the earliest examples is found in Genesis 18, where the "angel of the Lord" visits Abraham as one of three men. He shares a meal, foretells Isaac's birth, and discerns Sarah's hidden laughter—demonstrating both intimacy and omniscience. In Genesis 32, Jacob wrestles with a man until dawn, receiving a new name and a blessing. Jacob declares that he has seen God face to face, a moment of physical struggle that marks a profound spiritual transformation.

Other Christophanies echo this pattern. In Joshua 5, the commander of the Lord's army appears with a drawn sword, accepts worship, and instructs Joshua to remove his sandals—signs of divine authority. In Judges 6, the angel calls Gideon to lead Israel and ignites an offering with fire. In Judges 13, he announces Samson's birth and ascends in flames after receiving a sacrifice. These encounters are not mere visions—they are relational engagements that affirm identity, commission purpose, and elicit worship. Even in quieter moments, Christ's presence is unmistakable. In 1 Kings 19, an angel sustains Elijah with food for forty days.

Today, I no longer look for Christophanies in the form of Old Testament appearances. Instead, I recognize Christ's ongoing presence through the Holy Spirit, as promised in Matthew 28:20, "I am with you always." This is not a temporary visitation but a permanent indwelling. I sense Him in worship when a hymn stirs conviction. I see Him in service, when helping others brings unexpected joy, echoing John 14:21. In trials, scriptures like Isaiah 41:10 speak directly to my heart. At times, dreams or quiet impressions offer direction, as in Acts 2:17.

These moments are not as dramatic as my initial apparition of Jesus, but they still reveal Christ's ever-present, gentle, and guiding character. They teach me to listen, to respond, and to refine the contours of my daily life in a way that pleases God.